WealthTech: Wealth and Asset Management in the FinTech Age

WealthTech: Wealth and Asset Management in the FinTech Age

Edited by

Patrick Schueffel

INFORMATION AGE PUBLISHING, INC.
Charlotte, NC • www.infoagepub.com

Library of Congress Cataloging-In-Publication Data

The CIP data for this book can be found on the Library of Congress website (loc.gov).

Paperback: 978-1-64113-848-2
Hardcover: 978-1-64113-849-9
eBook: 978-1-64113-850-5

Printed in the United States of America

CONTENTS

PART 3

SOCIETAL TRENDS AFFECTING WEALTH & ASSET MANAGEMENT

PART 4

IT MANAGEMENT, DATA PRIVACY AND REGULATORY IMPLICATIONS

PART 5

FINANCIAL RISK AND PERFORMANCE MEASUREMENT

PREFACE

Patrick Schueffel

Digital transformation is creating game-changing opportunities and disruptions across industries and businesses. One industry where these game-changing opportunities will have profound impacts is wealth and asset management. For generations, wealth and asset management was a privileged service provided to co-operations and wealthy individuals. The informational advantages that wealth managers held vis-à-vis their clients provided a key competitive differentiator. In the current digital transformation climate, this differentiator is vanishing, and the setting is changing. A top priority on the agenda for any wealth and asset manager must therefore be how to respond and prepare for the ramifications of this fast-changing business environment. Thanks to the 25 contributions by 34 thought leaders of the asset and wealth management industry, this book provides the reader with a head-start in adapting to this new digital environment.

This volume is intended as the primary resource for the wealth and asset management technology revolution. It examines the rise of financial technology and its growing impact on the wealth and asset management industry. Written by industry experts in the global WealthTech space, this book offers an analysis of the current tectonic shifts happening in wealth and asset management and aggregates diverse industry expertise into a single informative volume. It examines the rise of financial technology and its growing impact on the wealth and asset management industry and is intended to provide practitioners such as wealth managers, bankers and investors with the answers they need to capitalize on this lucrative

WealthTech: Wealth and Asset Management in the FinTech Age, pages ix–xii.

market. As a primer on WealthTech it furthermore offers academics clear insight into the repercussions of profoundly changing business models. It additionally highlights the concept of the ongoing democratization of wealth management towards a more efficient and client-centric advisory process, free of entry hurdles.

Aggregating facts, expertise, insights and acumen from many authors, this book strives to answer questions such as: Who are key players in WealthTech? What is fueling its exponential growth? What are the key technologies behind WealthTech? How do regulators respond? What are the risks? What is the reaction of incumbent players?

The wealth and asset management industry is facing a number of significant challenges: macro-economic pressures, market environment volatility, increasing and tighter regulations, rising cost structures, changes in client behavior and a changing client landscape, and, new entrants to the market. Wealth and asset managers must adjust to the "new realities". Further complicating these challenges are new technical developments entering the industry.

The digitalization of the financial industry is displaying disruptive features which will have major implications for the entire wealth and asset management sector. Two facets of this disruption are particularly interesting: first, the qualitative changes of the wealth and asset management service (Will a Robo-advisor provide better advise than a human? What about the trust component?) and secondly, qualitative changes in the wealth and asset management industry (Can more people now receive wealth management services than before? Can asset management be provided more cost-efficiently?).

I sincerely believe that FinTech marks the beginning of a new era for the wealth and asset management industry. New technological trends in wealth and asset management, are shaking up the industry. In fact, on its own account WealthTech can now be defined as a new domain within the financial industry that applies technology to improve wealth management and private banking. Currently, the effects of these developments and their ramifications are unclear, and the path ahead is even less visible. This book will aim to fill the current knowledge gap in this area by addressing both of these elements. It is structured along the following 10 parts:

1. Introduction
   A tour d'horizon on FinTech and its impact on asset and wealth management will be provided along with a few critical remarks in this first chapter
2. Technological Trends Affecting Wealth & Asset Management
   Numerous technological trends that affect wealth & asset management will be discussed: From so called Open APIs which facilitate communication among organizations, to Big Data that allows for new types of services and different marketing approaches, to distributed ledgers such as

the Blockchain, and digital assets such as virtual currencies—a plethora of new technologies will be touched upon.

3. Societal Trends Affecting Wealth & Asset Management
    Millennials are a new client segment that wealth managers will have to address and accommodate. New service offerings as well as sales processes and channels will be required. Wealth management will be democratized as offerings will not only become cheaper and but also more widely available. All of these topics and more will be discussed in this chapter.

4. IT & Risk Management, Data Privacy and Regulatory Implications
    With a wider spread of online wealth management services among new client segments, the breadth of IT management will also increase. In this chapter it will be discussed how IT security can be enhanced and data privacy ensured. Moreover, new WealthTech offerings often do not fit into the traditional schemes of regulators. Enhancement of regulations will be required. This chapter will therefore elaborate how matters such data privacy and the reaction of regulators to the latest WealthTech trends.

5. Financial Risk and Performance Measurement
    WealthTech will confront decision makers with entirely new question concerning risk and performance management as Robo-advisors may soon manage large shares of pension funds. The contributing authors discuss these and related topics in this chapter.

6. The Competitive Landscape
    The emergence of new WealthTech offerings will produce changing dynamics in the competitive landscape among market incumbents as well as creating new market entrants. Here we will examine the future development of the asset and wealth management industry not only by naming these players, but also by hypothesizing potential effects on those wealth and asset management services.

7. The Wider Value Chain
    WealthTech will not only affect banks but will also have ramifications along the entire wealth and asset management value chain. It will be highlighted in book chapter how asset managers may use WealthTech, what impacts the adjustment to WealthTech may have on partners in the value chain.

8. Product Development and Innovation
    Innovation processes and product development will undergo substantial change as technology changes. Innovation cycles will become shorter and the wealth and asset management industry must get prepared for more disruptive rather than incremental innovations. Open innovation may be a suitable response to that challenge and is discussed here along with related issues.

9. Marketing and Sales

    Along with technological and societal changes, wealth and asset managers must reconsider their market segmentation strategies. New client acquisition processes will become necessary along with different frameworks for customer relationship management. New public relations strategies must be considered in the age of social media and viral marketing.

10. The Human side of WealthTech

    As WealthTech brings substantial change to the wealth and asset management industry, there will also be a significant impact on the human side of the business. Accordingly, the human resource function in organizations will undergo substantial changes and education and training programs in investment topics must be adapted to address and prepare for the new reality. Research and development at universities and other research facilities will also need to adjust to the WealthTech theme and are treated in this chapter.

The editor would like to express his gratitude to all contributors who helped make this book a reality. I am furthermore deeply indebted to our publishers at Information Age Publishing Inc. for their patience. Despite the best efforts of all contributors, however, I must accept responsibility for all remaining shortcomings. I hope that the value the reader finds in reading this book compensates for these limitations.

—*Patrick Schueffel, Editor*
WealthTech: Wealth and Asset Management in the FinTech Age

PART 1

INTRODUCTION

CHAPTER 1

DIGITIZING WEALTH MANAGEMENT

The Opportunity That Turns Into a Threat

Marc P. Bernegger

Wealth management is a very traditional and lucrative business that, compared with other financial services, has been little influenced by digitization. However, the advance of sophisticated technologies and changing customer needs are two reasons why the industry will soon be subject to some major changes.

The volume of assets that are managed by asset and wealth management firms globally has increased rapidly over the last few years. The industry's forecasts predict that the strong growth will continue. However, while the advance of new technologies and innovation caused a paradigm shift in large parts of the financial services industry, the effects on asset and wealth management (AWM) have not been very strong.

The need for digitization of services has been negligible. Customer needs were a driving factor in the development of digital financial services, but not so for AWM. Compared to the core business to consumer (B2C) services of traditional banks and insurers, the total number of clients is much smaller. Furthermore, there are fewer interaction points: High net worth individuals as well as larger com-

WealthTech: Wealth and Asset Management in the FinTech Age, pages 3–6.

panies contract asset managers in order to take a passive position. This does not necessarily mean that customer experience is not important in the AWM segment, but it is not a deal breaker. There have not been extensive frontends or applications that millions of customers were using on a daily basis. For AWM clients, the performance was and still is crucial.

The industry is a very traditional one: Clients seek personal relationships. When you entrust someone with valuable assets you want to know who is managing them, and what those managers' track records are. These relationships were also important in daily B2C financial services once but are not considered by the majority of people today when they select a bank in order to open an account or apply for credit. Thus, although it occurred in almost every other part of the financial industry, what reason has been there for change in AWM? None!

WealthTech companies are being launched and aim to reshape the AWM industry in several fields: Robo-advisory, investing tools, digital brokerage, portfolio management, and other areas are subject to innovation and digitization, driven by newly founded companies that substitute some of the traditional service providers.

Although I stated that clients would primarily seek personal relationships with those people whom they entrust with their assets, customers' needs have drastically changed within the last few years. People became accustomed to all the advantages brought into their daily lives by digitization. Flexibility, agility and usability already reshaped a vast amount of services that once were analog. Apps and mobile devices do not necessarily eliminate the need for personal interaction, but they do change the way the interaction works. While in certain markets, such as the insurance industry, big players work relentlessly on improving their frontends in order to satisfy customers, many AWM businesses still do not even have a digital front-end. For clients however, customer experience and usability have become factors that are equally important to the pricing of services and while 69 % of high net worth individuals (HNWIs) are using online financial services, only 25 % of asset and wealth managers currently offer digital channels other than email.[1] That is why startups such as Elinvar were founded, to change the look and feel of AWM by creating digital interfaces. It's clear that the future of the AWM industry will be determined by how well providers adapt to the changes brought by digitization.

The pricing of services will still matter. The possibility of easily comparing products and services on price is another consequence of the all-embracing digitization trend. That is why prices and returns must be even more competitive. In that context, Robo-advisory is about to change the AWM game. Artificial intelligence will be able to manage assets much more efficiently and at a lower cost, providing more profit to managers as well as customers. Although fintech companies such as Scalable Capital already offer investment services based on Robo-advise, automation is only in the fledgling stages. Investments will be made fully automated based on self-learning algorithms. The automated services of the future are more than just advise. We can expect fully automated portfolio management within the next decade, providing higher efficiency and transparency.

Still, it is unlikely that these automated AWM solutions will substitute traditional players any time soon. As mentioned before, the industry is a traditional one and customer relations are eminently important. Thus, the combination of long-established consultation and innovative technology is the most likely result of both approaches merging.

WHAT CONSEQUENCES CAN BE EXPECTED?

According to recent reports, the volume of managed assets in the AWM industry will continue to grow. Especially in Asia and to a certain extent also in Africa strong economic growth will increase the need for AWM services. The industry will therefore remain a highly lucrative business. However, the market landscape will change. There will be a consolidation that concerns both traditional wealth management companies and WealthTech startups. Adjusting to cost pressures, the sprouting digital environment and newly evolving customer needs will be key to success.

The question that remains is, when will these consequences become visible? In retail banking, digitization advanced very quickly after big players started to introduce online banking services. In addition, most services have been made accessible via mobile devices in the last couple of years after smartphones created the need for services to be digitally delivered.

Now, major wealth managers are working on the implementation of Robo-advisors[2] and already two years ago, more than 30 % of wealth managers were planning to offer certain services for mobile devices.[3]

The AWM industry is at the same point that retail banking was roughly 10 years ago. Not every wealth manager believes in the opportunities of offering digital services, but the majority are aware of the fact that the future is indeed a digital one. On one side, some wealth management companies will successfully transform their services and products, while some will fail and presumably disappear. On the other side, even more WealthTech startups will step into the market to participate in the industry's change by developing new technology-based applications and services. Some of them will be acquired by big players in the industry, some may establish themselves to become a lead player and others will fail to make an impact and disappear again. The bottom line is that the wealth management landscape will certainly look different in two or three years, and the digitization that once was an opportunity, is transforming into a threat for those that do not respond to the changes that are happening around them.

REFERENCES

1. *Sink or swim: Why wealth management can't afford to miss the digital wave.* Retrieved from: https://www.pwc.com/sg/en/publications/assets/wealth-20-sink-or-swim-ap.pdf
2. *The expansion of robo-advisory in wealth management.* Retrieved from: https://www2.deloitte.com/content/dam/Deloitte/de/Documents/financial-services/Deloitte-Robo-safe.pdf
3. *Asset and wealth management trends.* Retrieved from: https://www.pwc.com/gx/en/ceo-survey/2019/Theme-assets/reports/ceo-survey-2019-asset-wealth-management.pdf

CHAPTER 2

IS FINTECH A RED HERRING?

J. P. Caldeira

The topic of FinTech is increasingly popular throughout the financial world. Yet, this catch phrase and its heavy focus on technology should not distract us from more fundamental problems faced by customers and the needs they want to have satisfied.

Technology is just a means to an end, not the end in itself. Nevertheless, through the history of mankind, technology has changed the life of millions either by increasing efficiency or by pushing the boundaries of what is possible. In doing so has it disrupted innumerable businesses and sometimes entire industries that could not or would not adapt to the new paradigm.

FinTech is not different. The current FinTech wave of innovation has essentially been fueled by two technological breakthroughs that together have changed the way most of us behave and interact with others, be it persons or companies. The first is the general availability of smart phones or other mobile devices and of broadband wireless Internet connections. The second one is the dramatic reduction of the cost of computing power.

These two factors together allow those who harness their possibilities to develop new models of client interaction attain a significant cost-advantage or even create completely new business models that disrupt the existing ones. But in the end, it will be customer satisfaction with the service provided that will separate the winners from the losers, not the technology used. In most of the cases, the

WealthTech: Wealth and Asset Management in the FinTech Age, pages 7–8.

customer does not buy a technology. He or she buys a product or a service with specific characteristics that have value for them.

This may sound trivial and obvious, but there are many examples out there that prove that managers have sometimes lost track of this simple fact. Just think about "Internet-banking" in the Web 1.0 era of the early 2000's and the current hype about "Robo-advisory", " Machine-learning" or "Artificial Intelligence". In fact, those are often misunderstood by those who use them and designate the "trees" but hide the forest. Buzzwords are used that potentially distract us from the real issues at hand.

Customer do not want to know or care about if it is an algorithm or a "robot" that manages his/ her investments. What he/she really cares about is a way to get access to an affordable, cost-efficient, and unbiased investment management that allows him or her to attain his long-term financial goals.

Today it is hard to find an offer from a traditional vendor that fulfills all those requirements. Robo-advisory now promises to do just that, and its disruptive power comes not from the technology itself but from the fact that it fills a value-vacancy.

In theory this could be done either by a new-entrant (typically a start-up) or an incumbent (typically a private bank). Yet, there are two preconditions for an incumbent to be able to be sufficiently agile to beat a start-up in filling this vacancy.

The first is that it has the necessary skills to do it, i.e. that it CAN do it. I am not speaking only of technological skills that at the end of the day can be acquired in the market. The most important factor is the organizational skills that are required to execute and deliver innovation. Banks are designed and wired to assure flawless execution and control risks, but not to be agile and to innovate. It is embedded in their structure, systems, corporate culture, regulatory framework and so on. It is intrinsically difficult to actually create an ambidextrous banking organization that is both excellent at execution and at outstanding in banking. But is not impossible and the trend for business process outsourcing and the emergence of pure-play transactional banks might become an important enabler for that.

The second preconditions for a traditional bank be able to successfully compete with a FinTech startup is that it WANTS to do it. This is the more difficult one to comply with, for in many cases it involves significant changes in the established way of doing business and potentially even cannibalizing oneself. And for this to happen, top management has to swiftly acquire a true understanding of what "FinTechs" really stands for which goes well beyond buzzwords or techno-lingo. More importantly, top management must also understand how it can contribute to better serving the customer giving him and her "more for less".

Rest assured that if do not do it somebody else will, and it might not even be a FINTECH.

CHAPTER 3

FINTECH: THE GENIE WILL NOT TURN BACK TO HIS BOTTLE

Raphael Cretinon and Jean Bonnefoy

A study conducted by Pericles Consulting in 2017 shows that 71% of prominent assets managers collaborate with startups and FinTechs. As traditional financial services players need to continuously adapt their product and service offerings to align with the rapid pace of sociological and technological changes, FinTechs can offer smart solutions which accelerate the time to market through "turnkey" innovations based on new technologies. Moreover, innovation management and the range of collaboration models with FinTechs are appealing factors for investment and wealth management companies alike.

WHAT IS A FINTECH FIRM?

A FinTech firm is a company that provides new financial services or solutions to financial actors, based on new technologies such as Blockchain, Big Data, Machine Learning or provides business processes digitalization. Usually, FinTechs have been created around a business process in order to make it simpler, faster, and cheaper.

These new players to the financial industry have experienced a significant growth in recent years, particularly in Europe and Asia. For example, there were 111 FinTechs in Switzerland in 2015 compared with around 350 companies today.

WealthTech: Wealth and Asset Management in the FinTech Age, pages 9–13.
Copyright © 2020 by Information Age Publishing

9

Global investment in FinTechs increased fivefold between 2016 and 2018 and totaled USD 111.8bn in 2018. FinTech has become a large playground for investors who are convinced by the potential of the digital transformation of the banking and insurance sectors. FinTechs are becoming mainstream in large part due to B2C (business-to-consumer) offerings such as alternative payment systems, Robo-advisors and crowd funding/lending platforms. A 2017 survey has shown that the average percentage of digitally active consumers using FinTech services reached 33% across the 20 markets surveyed (30% in Switzerland). However, the success of some of these B2C FinTechs is overshadowing the wide range of creative and attractive B2B (business-to-business) offers.

FROM COMPETITION TO COOPERATION

The pinnacle of the FinTechs is considered by many to be PayPal, the now popular company of secure online payment solutions founded in 1998. The PayPal solution was designed as a competitor to other instant cash transfer systems which were being developed by banks.

The first FinTech generation was born out of the aftermath of the 2008 financial crisis. As a result of many financial and banking institutions being forced to restructure or close, executives and top managers found themselves having to reassess their career options. Some used this as an opportunity to design new innovative products and reshape the client experience which had a significant impact on the financial services industry. This wave of newcomers with a "Silicon Valley" management style (no more tie and jacket) used technology to propose products and services that directly competed with the traditional bankers. Until recently, there was talk in the market about the "uberization" of finance. Some said that FinTechs would disrupt banks. This mindset has now changed.

Many FinTechs have turned their focus towards B2B offerings, integrating their solution into the value chain of the traditional actors. These financial start-ups have realized that retail customer acquisition and heavy industry regulations produces barrier to entry.

A TIME FOR ENHANCED COOPERATION
BETWEEN THE OLD AND THE NEW

The second generation of FinTechs is more frequently positioned in the B2B or B2B2C market, partnering their innovative digital solutions with the traditional financial service providers.

The best example of this is the "pivot" of FinTechs who provide Robo-advisory technology. It can be described as a "pivot" because Robo-advisors first targeted to serve the retail client directly. Today, most European Robo-advisors collaborate with banks and insurance companies to service retail clients. The automation of investments allocations based on customer profiling combined with the digitalization of the client experience are highly sought after by wealth managers. The technology improves the client interaction experience while reducing the advisory costs and enabling financial solutions to be provided to the retail market which were previously only offered to the high net worth clients.

TECHNOLOGY AS A SOLUTION TO REGULATORY HYPERINFLATION IN THE FINANCIAL SECTOR

Entrepreneurs understand that business risks can also create tremendous business opportunities. RegTechs illustrate this phenomenon well.

The strict regulatory environment in the financial services sector creates an increasingly heavy- compliance burden for the industry players. Reputational risk is also a key factor. Industry participants are willing to pay for affordable solutions that address regulatory compliance requirements. Technology produces several benefits to the compliance field. First of all, the technology allows the production of comprehensive audit trails in areas of transactions, advise, and client interactions. For example, "Qumram" captures and stores digital activity and interactions with clients.

Technology also facilitates the KYC (Know Your Customer) legal requirements. An example here is the startup "KYC3" which simplifies the due diligence and Anti Money Laundering process and helps companies get interactive reports to take decisions. Regtech can also ease other legal obligations. Since 2013, French Insurers are obliged to detect unclaimed contracts and to do everything possible to identify the recipient. "Mister Doe" is positioned in this market providing algorithms of data quality control, allowing the detection unclaimed contracts.

INNOVATION MANAGEMENT, A KEY FACTOR

How do banking institutions manage this innovation revolution? Historical global giants have collapsed due to their failure in innovation (KODAK, NOKIA, Blackberry). Market leaders can become business case failures due to a lack of innovation. Innovation management has become a key challenge for all companies, including financial services companies.

Today there exists an innovation management deficit in the financial services sector even where companies have integrated digital transformation into their strategic plans. European banks are struggling to be able adapt quickly to the n customer requirements and expectations. This is in part a legacy problem where the core banking system of many major banks is still supported by old programing languages such as Cobol which represent a strong constraint to the evolution of these systems. It is very complicated, time consuming, and costly to bring those systems up to latest technology standards. This legacy issue prevents these firms from being as agile as a neobank.

Many companies are focused on optimizing the customer experience by revisiting their current service offerings. BBVA is ranked No. 1, according to Forrester, for the best user experience with its mobile application which was developed in close proximity with FinTechs and inspired by the model of neobanks like N26. In addition to its functionality, the application stands out for its simplicity. Any user can choose his/her mode of interaction.

Unfortunately, innovation is not a concept which can be mandated. It must be part of the corporate culture. An innovation culture has a profound impact on the organization structure; it changes governance, flattens hierarchies, eliminates silo operations. One just need to look at Google or Facebook to observe this.

For many European banks, the current operations model does not allow the evolvement of innovation. It is necessary to entrench innovation at the heart of the company's strategy and have the full support of the board. There are several approaches financial organizations can adopt to integrate innovation into their organizational set-up and product and service offering.

At the same time not one primary model for innovation management should be considered, but a range of guidelines. Let us take as a first example the "Banque de France", which has paved the way since 2016 with the appointment of a Chief Digital Officer and the creation of a "Lab". The purpose is to develop Blockchain as a tool for financial authorities. In this case, the aim is to integrate innovation into the structure. The result of this strategy remains to be seen.

Another example is Axa, which has created a startup innovation-based ecosystem with "Kamet" an incubator, Axa Strategic Ventures dedicated to investments in technologies that shape the future of insurance and asset-management and Axa Digital Partnerships that builds long term partnerships with startups.

Other platforms for innovation include "hackathons", which are open-innovation platforms where companies invite employees to work with customers, students, consultants and/or startups. Intrapreneurship is another concept for innovation where employees develop in-house solutions autonomously and with a dedicated budget.

Whatever form of innovation is realized, the time to market (T2M) is essential and will ultimately determine whether or not the innovation is a success.

The multi-year planning of projects is no longer in line with the pace of market developments which has accelerated considerably. However, we must differentiate "Front End" innovation (visible by customer) where the T2M is critical, from the "Back End" innovation which tends to be slower given the legacy systems require considerable effort to be replaced.

The cooperation between incumbent organizations and startups should accelerate the T2M of innovation. However, it should be noted that the decision-making time for startup organizations (often a few weeks) is typically not aligned with the decision-making time of the incumbent organizations (often several months). Both parties must adapt their styles to learn to work with each other.

CONCLUSION

The genie will not turn back to his bottle. The FinTech offer is real and will shape future strategy. These new organizations are actively participating in the acceleration of the digital transformation of the financial sector. The key will be how the incumbent organizations work with the FinTechs. Approaches to this collaboration can vary widely: from service provider or supplier to acquisition or strategic partnership.

An acquisition of startups could be a trigger that would potentially kill the startup innovation capacity depending on the integration strategy of the incumbent company. Innovation comes from creativity that comes from freedom. The recommended option is the "English Garden" allegory which let the startup flourish while providing the required funding and strong business support.

In the end, the customer will be the judge. Innovation must serve the needs of the customer.

PART 2

TECHNOLOGICAL TRENDS AFFECTING WEALTH & ASSET MANAGEMENT

CHAPTER 4

INFORMATION STRATEGY IN A CHANGING LANDSCAPE OF INVESTMENT MANAGEMENT

Nicolas Buerkler and Helena Steiner

Since the 1980s, the financial sector has been characterized by credit expansion, changes in regulation, decoupling of the financial sector from the real economy, and decreasing interest rates leading to a relaxing of credit standards, inefficient allocation of capital, and inflated asset prices. Given the market conditions, it was rather easy to have comfortable returns on an average portfolio, leading to the belief that following market trends will lead to successful investments. In today's environment of low or negative yields, investment managers can no longer rely on the established valuation methods metrics of the past. Contemporary investment managers face many difficulties within the financial sector such as high stock market valuations, low yielding bonds, expensive real estate markets and slowing economic growth. The wider socio-economic outlook is just as bleak, with the slow erosion of purchasing power of middle-class consumers, rising poverty rates, political instability, and unsustainable governmental debts. The socio-political implications of these symptoms often coincide with the increasing "financialization" of a society, rising inequality, and subsequent manipulation of media for government or corporate interests.

WealthTech: Wealth and Asset Management in the FinTech Age, pages 17–22.

17

MANIPULATION IN MEDIA AND GOVERNMENTAL DATA

The media normally seeks to maintain an image of impartiality and accuracy in journalism, why then would it consent to being manipulated? The obvious answer is that they are owned and controlled by larger interest groups, from both the public and private sector, who seek to maintain control over the populace through mainstream media outlets for the furthering of their own agenda and ideologies and to maintain the status quo. It is well known that the vast majority of mainstream media outlets are owned or controlled by a few institutions or individuals.

Nearly all published information is influenced by some dominant ideology or personal views, which is usually motivated by a political or economic outlook. The financial sector is especially prone to this sort of media manipulation due to its importance as an indicator of the vitality of a nation and to portray an image of attractive investment opportunities.

Governments will often publicize skewed data to portray their success in attaining financial power and economic stability, and ignore the problems caused by increased inequality, and uneven distribution of wealth and the gains of increased productivity. Large corporations will use their political power to influence policy makers in adopting regulations that benefit their business model or competitive advantage. Influential investment managers use their popularity to convince their followers to buy or sell certain assets, and profit from the market movements.

As political or economic instability rises, manipulation becomes more obvious and increasingly inaccurate and useless information will be published, in an attempt to avoid civil unrest, and reassure the populace that everything is under control and working toward the interests of the people. Investment managers should ensure their knowledge base consists of diverse sources which can help to qualify the information being reported, and ensure the conclusions are as close to reality as possible and avoid the risks associated with manipulated information. To achieve this, it is not enough to simply read alternative news sources from the same socio-political areas of the world, it is also vital to understand how opposing government's view contemporary issues, and how local media sources report on these issues to their own audiences. Being able to read the news in two or more languages can increase the accuracy of conclusions by a significant margin as the expressions used will offer key insights into what is "really" going on, rather than what the media wants people to believe.

Thanks to the increasing diversity of opinions in the international media channels and the internet granting instant access to a wide range of alternative news providers, the lack of quality in mainstream media can be more than compensated for. In order to gain the most benefits, a selected variety of sources should be carefully investigated for quality, diversity of opinion, regional outlooks, and a combination of traditional, expert, and specialist sources. The images in Figure 4.1 show an example of how media outlets can be mapped. Since it is unrealistic to assume one can follow all channels effectively, the highest quality of each sector should be selected with the variances on standard to alternative.

FIGURE 4.1. Financial Media and Their Ideological Biases (http://www.sim-re-search.ch/meinungen/SI%20news%20maps.pdf)

In summary, rational investment is about informed decision making and can only be as good as the information which backs it. Investment managers' prime directive should be to ensure that the information base is as high-quality, accurate, and diverse as possible, making sure to take into account expert and specialist knowledge, not just traditional sources.

KEY COMPONENTS OF SUCCESSFUL INVESTMENT MANAGEMENT

A well-rounded investment strategy should consist of a clear methodology for access and handling opportunities, a theoretical framework, and a clear information strategy:

1. Operation: Structure, processes, access, and procedure
2. Framework: Models and theories for evaluation, analysis, and decisions
3. Strategy: Information, influencing data, investment access

Most investment activity focuses on operations and frameworks, both of which have received a lot of focus in recent history, to the point where there is little that can be improved or that has not already been implemented. Since most investment managers have adopted the same principles, based on the Modern Portfolio Theory, and the Capital Asset Pricing Models, this limits the effectiveness of any single investment and reduces the competitive edge that could be obtained by a better analysis of the information available and adopting alternative strategies.

The investment manager who wants to explore alternative markets and non-common investments, would require a more holistic approach to using information to build strategies. This approach requires more time to be invested in the collection and structuring of information, but the rewards are well worth the effort of diverging from the highly capitalized standard markets. To adopt this type of holistic approach to investment strategies, it is vital for investment managers to understand the types of knowledge that are available, and to have an understanding of the strengths and weaknesses of each, and how they can best be implemented within the investment framework.

TYPOLOGY OF KNOWLEDGE WITHIN INFORMATION MANAGEMENT

Knowledge can be broadly divided into three categories, surface knowledge, expert knowledge, and specialist knowledge. Each classification of knowledge has its own particular set of advantages and methodology for accessing and distilling it into a format that can be purposed towards the targeted outcomes.

Surface knowledge is widely available in large quantities, commonly referred to as Big Data. Where once big data was only accessible to large corporations, recent advances in AI have made it accessible to a wider number of fields and applications, widening its accessibility while simultaneously lowering its value.

Expert knowledge is a smaller set of data which is most often found in blogs written by specialists in a particular field, published as best practices, or in courses and educational materials. Expert knowledge offers key insights to topics which cannot be easily analyzed through AI algorithms or smart search engines, as the information is not of a sufficient volume to offer accurate and dependable insights into a given topic or area of research.

Specialist knowledge is the rarest of the types of knowledge. This knowledge exists primarily in the minds of the brightest experts of any given industry. The key element of specialist knowledge is that it has been built up over time, allowing a historical linkage between knowledge of events as they were in the past, to assessing predictable trends to events as they exist now. Specialist knowledge is a highly valuable resource to have at one's disposal that is unavailable to the vast majority of investment managers and can quickly set apart the holders of this knowledge as the thought-leaders and forward thinkers in the industry.

THE CONCEPT OF AN INFORMATION MANAGEMENT SYSTEM

Turning specialist knowledge into expert knowledge is key to a successful investment strategy, building a well-balanced portfolio, and providing in-depth evidence for each investment opportunity. The accumulation of specialist knowledge should be diverse enough to apply to a variety of scenarios and investment opportunities while retaining its relevance to the complex systems in which investments models and concepts are carried out. The knowledge itself also offers a key strategic advances to the holders, as it is both expensive and difficult to accumulate, making it highly sought after.

Information Management Systems (IMS) offer the unique opportunity of bringing together specialist and expert knowledge from a wide variety of sources into a single platform where the information can be easily structured and analyzed for future investment opportunities or repackaged as anecdotal evidence to be shared with clients. The technology is focused on a more holistic approach to data modelling, using Smart Technologies to provide the flexibility needed to quickly analyze trends in both highly volatile markets which are primarily driven by short-term investment decisions, alongside the more long-term participation investments.

Traditional data models typically analyze information within narrowly defined models, requiring the investment manager to define the topic and desired parameters within which to source an answer, often at the expense of losing key insights if the topic is too narrowly defined. IMS', on the other hand, are designed to avoid this issue by allowing both in-depth analysis within a particular framework, while retaining an overall link to the wider information base.

This allows the information to be efficiently repurposed to a wide variety of potential investment opportunities and to the discovery of new trends outside the scope of traditional financial media sources. Another benefit of IMS' is the capability to provide insights with smaller data sets, allowing investment managers to glean insights quickly, and readjust the outputs efficiently with each new piece of information.

This flexibility is important in order to provide for both current needs which are known, and future needs which are as yet unknown. This constant updating of the interconnected bits of data provides a relatively fast method for investment managers to analyze where new links are being created, and older ones retired, maintaining a constant level of quality within the IMS as it is fed more recent and relevant information.

For systems where the data model has to allow adaptability, interconnectivity, self-learning, and flexibility, a holistic data model is best suited towards this purpose, especially when expert and specialist knowledge are a primary source of information, in addition to high-quality news media sources.

IMPLEMENTING IMS TO MAKE INVESTMENT MANAGEMENT READY FOR THE FUTURE

Most initiatives to bring technology into the investment field are focused on using big data with the hope of improving investment decisions. Unfortunately, this does not take into account the potential manipulation of the sources of information or guarantee that alternative views are presented.

In order to meet the challenges of a manipulated data, an investment manager should adopt an Information Management System that allows data to be classified, not only by topic or theme, but also to help flag potentially manipulated sources and provide the investment managers with alternative sources to balance the information.

In a competitive market, investment managers with the capability of recognizing and finding new investment opportunities before they become mainstream gives them a competitive edge. In order to achieve this, there has to be the right information available at the right moment. To secure these requirements, a system must be implemented which enables strategic decision making, anticipates changes and has the flexibility to adapt to them.

IMS' based on Smart Technologies offer a unique way for information managers to gather information from a variety of standard and alternative sources, collaborate with selected specialists to create proprietary expert knowledge, in a platform designed to structure information into a useable format with the flexibility to readjust connection between diverse information clusters creating a unique information pool, which will enable them to stay at the forefront of investment decisions.

Such Information-driven strategies are already being adopted by a leading independent Hong Kong based investment management company, with further applications being tested in the Swiss market.

CHAPTER 5

WEALTHTECH—THE BRAVE NEW WORLD?

Alexander Tomenendal

WealthTech holds promise for various areas of the financial industry. This contribution discusses how latest technological trends will affect the development of WealthTech. For this purpose, an entire array of technologies will be discussed, including Artificial Intelligence, Big Data, Blockchain, Cloud Services, Gamification, Microtransactions, Open APIs, Robotic Process Automation, Smart Contracts, Social Networks, and Virtual Currencies. The question will be investigated whether this nexus of technologies will create the brave new world of WealthTech.

INTRODUCTION

Current trends in FinTech are often competing. Yet, on occasion these trends also complement each other. When looking at each technology trend individually it is not obvious what a world may look like, where all those trends come together. However, this thought experiment provides a foundation for a holistic view on the future of WealthTech. The implications are not only relevant for the main players in the industry, but also society as a whole.

The key trends that will be addressed in this article are Artificial Intelligence, Big Data, Blockchain, Cloud Services, Gamification, Microtransactions, Open APIs, Robotic Process Automation, Smart Contracts, Social Networks, and Virtu-

WealthTech: Wealth and Asset Management in the FinTech Age, pages 23–33.
Copyright © 2020 by Information Age Publishing
All rights of reproduction in any form reserved.

al Currencies. Each of these trends has some obvious consequences and extrapolating their effects gives us a more vivid outlook on the things to come.

When considering all effects simultaneously, a comprehensive picture emerges. For some this picture may be intimidating, others may find it exciting. In any case, it is a future much different from the present.

ARTIFICIAL INTELLIGENCE (AI)

The name 'Artificial Intelligence' holds a lot of promise. Nevertheless, it is far from what could be considered 'Human Intelligence'. Current AI is pretty useless when it comes to creativity. Give an AI machine a blank sheet of paper and ask it to brainstorm to create an investment strategy and it will fall short. It is still very dependent on humans to provide context and measurements for success. However, once this context is available, AIs outperform humans significantly as they can spot patterns in huge, complex data. They can diligently dig through an immense number of scenarios. In addition, they can run simulations at a rate that outclasses human intuition by sheer brute force. Combined, this destines AI for Wealth and Asset Management. As context is easily established for an AI, it can then quickly devise, test and execute investment strategies that would take highly specialized analyst days or even weeks to come up with. As the average life time of these strategies is also just measured in days or weeks, AI can quickly shift gears when profitability drops.

BIG DATA

Big Data delivers on the promise to not just stockpile huge amounts of data, but also to be able to effectively work with that data. It combines low level systems to organize and store data with advances in hardware in storage technology. On top of that, a set of tools and procedures has emerged that can work on these huge data sets. Data itself is typically available cheaply and in abundance. Transforming this data into actionable information is still a major challenge. Big Data is an enabling technology that provides the means to store large amounts of data but also the performance needed to efficiently scan, analyze and structure this data into meaningful information. Without Big Data, the other powerful technologies such as AI cannot achieve their full potential.

BLOCKCHAIN

To talk about Blockchain in 2019 still has the nasty ring to it of playing buzzword bingo. Too many ventures put a Blockchain sticker on their products when it is very unclear how Blockchain improves their products. At the same time the technology underlying Blockchain represents too much of a paradigm shift to be ignored when looking at the future of WealthTech. The most significant impact of Blockchain is that it can eliminate human intervention from transaction processing. With the correct credentials, any piece of software can enter into a binding transaction that is final. There is no ambiguity. There is also no reversal. This completely levels the playing field for algorithms. Whereas beforehand algorithms required human approval or run the risk of having their decisions overturned, these programs can now work autonomously. Humans at the same time can monitor and understand the ongoing processes, but they can no longer interfere once a trade is made. This eliminates most of the effort and time from current transactions. It also introduces new operational risks that destroy holdings at the blink of an eye without any technical or legal way of reversing the action.

CLOUD SERVICES

Standalone, Cloud Services are not much of an influence on wealth management itself. Rather, they disrupt how wealth management providers organize and run their businesses. Compared to classical infrastructure, Cloud Services are much easier to set up, reducing the investment hurdle for providers significantly and opening the market for new players. Services provided using the cloud can also become smaller and more granular, which puts more focus on interoperability of the components than on the comprehensiveness of a monolithic solution. It also better facilitates white-labeling. Cloud Services drive down software cost much like the App-Model has been undercutting prices of software packages. Finally, Cloud Services provide flexibility, where services are hosted, and allowing easy shifts for cost, regulatory or data privacy reasons.

GAMIFICATION

As a concept, Gamification has been around for a while, aiming to make business applications as much fun to use as computer games. Initially, the focus has been on how employees use a piece of software and it has turned to how clients are interacting with a service. But in this context it is less about how much 'fun' it is to interact with a wealth management service. Rather than that it is about what application developers can learn much from computer games on how to present complex situations and how to allow the users to make powerful, yet easy to understand decisions. Current strategy games are doing a much better job at this than any investment application. These strategy games offer us a view onto the future of user interface design.

MICROTRANSACTIONS

The acceptable or common size of a transaction varies much with the client and product segment. Payments and plain foreign exchange (FX) transaction mark the lower end of the scale, while highly complex products are only reasonable at four- or five-digit contract sizes. This is mostly due to the amount of human processing involved and the higher operational risk. While eliminating manual processing reduces the operational risk involved, it does not eliminate market risk, which would still set an effective boundary on how small transactions can get. Also, looking at very small transactions, there are 'quantum' effects: e.g. an FX transaction can only become as granular as the price interest point (PIP) size. Looking forward, the trend in dropping effective transaction sizes will continue and put margin-based business models in jeopardy. It will also allow investments to be much more adaptive to smaller changes in the market. With the improved capability of systems to keep track of complex investment portfolios, we will also experience better diversification of investments. Most importantly, it will open up market segments for Wealth Management that previously could not afford the entrance fee.

OPEN APIS

Open application programming interfaces (APIs) are a prerequisite for Cloud Services, modular applications, and Big Data sources to work together. Sometimes, standardization boards (attempt to) define these APIs. Moreover, are also de-facto standards of established APIs exist, such as Reuters Market Data Services. Lastly, there are APIs that are pragmatically defined by innovative FinTechs to fill an existing gap that has not been addressed so far. With evolutionary forces at play we can expect more powerful APIs to become available for many players in the financial services industry as well as clients. These APIs then eventually converge on those APIs that are merely good enough to solve a specific task. This evolution implies that application development will be less and less concerned with solving all problems in monolithic programs, but increasingly rely on existing services to fill gaps quicker, cheaper and better.

ROBOTIC PROCESS AUTOMATION (RPA)

In a nutshell, RPA allows employees to create scripted processing without major involvement of IT staff. It also provides version control and management of run-time environments that are necessary for production systems as opposed to stand-alone Excel scripts running on someone's desktop. As such, RPAs holds a lot of promise. In reality, RPAs are not quite as revolutionary, as projects still require dedicated RPA Business Analysts to create sensible scripts. Nevertheless, the number of people involved to move from business idea to production code can be significantly reduced. As such, RPA might further speed up development and reduce time to market for new applications. Although the concept is clear it remains to be seen whether the label RPA remains.

SMART CONTRACTS

Smart Contracts are typically associated with Blockchain technology. Yet, using the Blockchain is actually not a requirement. Any technology that equips software with sufficient levels of autonomy and authority could be the basis for smart contracts. What distinguishes a smart contract from a regular contract is that the entirety of the contractual agreements is codified in the smart contract. No additional considerations or exceptions exist beyond that. What is coded into the contract is all that there is. Machines can immediately understand and simulate these contracts. No further interpretation of the contract is required. Smart Contracts therefore do away with one of the most labor-intensive aspects of the current contracting system, namely investigating the differences between 'what was meant' by the contracting parties and 'what was written down'. Back-office staff and lawyers are no longer essential for settling contracts and disputes—with all the benefits and drawbacks this entails.

SOCIAL NETWORKS

How does the prospective investor build up trust into his investment advisor? Historically, we are looking at a sparse network with a single or at most a few advisors entrusted with the investment decision. Social Networks give an outlook on how this may look like in the future. It is safe to say that in future trust building will be less about how investors get in touch with advisors, but more about how investment applications connect with investment opportunities. Already today social networks facilitate trust building as well as information exchange and thereby help to grow beneficial relationships. In terms of relationships building, investment automation will then need to help the client to separate the wheat from the chaff. Whether these newly emerging relationships will form a network extending the current human social network or a separate network remains to be seen.

VIRTUAL CURRENCIES

As of 2019, the debate on virtual currencies (Bitcoin and Altcoins) is rather controversial. But regardless of the outcomes of this discussion, the concept of virtual currencies holds a promise that is too attractive to ignore. There has always been a need to account for items beyond goods which are priced in legal tender, such as airline miles, phone minutes, loyalty points etc. All those currencies have been around for decades. Virtual currencies allow a more transparent representation of a new type of money which is technically more stable and requires less manual administration overhead. The promise for wealth and asset management in this context, however, is less so seek another high risk/reward investment vehicle. Rather than that, wealth and asset management will benefit much from the means of immutable technological of asset accounting. Moreover, the ease by which a new virtual currency can be designed and emitted may yield dedicated currencies to support a single investment contract.

HOLISTIC ASPECTS IMPACTED
DIFFERENTLY BY CURRENT TRENDS

When considering the aforementioned technologies together, a comprehensive picture emerges. This will be illustrated by looking at the impact on key aspects of Wealth Management.

Trust—how trust is built and lost. And how fast. Over the past decades, it has been become ever easier to engage in business relationships, mostly due to the emergence of new technology but also due to cultural changes. But increased networking possibilities also brought along increased levels of risk. Fraud is easier to commit and becomes profitable at much lower levels. There is a constant battle between fraud prevention and new fraud schemes. As long as technical progress is constantly altering the playing field this battle is likely to continue. At the heart of this is the question of trust. Is an investment opportunity trustworthy enough to engage in? Whether the trust was justified is easy to establish after the fact. The challenge is that the investment decision needs to be made upfront. Trust is typically established through the facts of how well the involved parties are known, how clearly an investment contract is structured, and how dependable the investment technology is. AI is already and will become even better at spotting trustworthy patterns and learning from mistakes. The transparency of the Blockchain and Smart Contracts will reduce the level of trust required for transactions as crucial components will be increasingly verifiable—if you can validate the facts, no trust is necessary. Ultimately a bot-aware social network will allow to build trust and have reputations validated by communal judgement, rather than individual impressions. In the brave new WealthTech world, trust will be established much quicker, facts will be easier to verify but trust will also be lost very quickly in case of fraudulent behavior. With the difference between 'what was meant' versus 'what was written down' fading away over time, the nature of an investment decision will become more binding and therefore requires more trust on the part of the investor. Today, one can take the counterparty court when disagreeing on the interpretation of an agreement. Going forward, when a Smart Contract is triggered, there is virtually zero room for debate afterwards. This will pose a challenge for investors but especially to investment advisors as their reputation is on the line.

Usability—how easy are asset management services accessible? Complexity is a major barrier for sophisticated investment strategies. On a positive note, this aspect prevents investors from making investments into vehicles not understood. While this is positive when looking at the potential downsides of an investment product, it is burdensome if it emerges solely from a poor representation of the investment. What, however, if understanding could be made easier? The usability of products as well as asset management platforms will increase over time. As the IT industry is putting a stronger emphasis on user experience lately improved analysis capabilities will also help to make complex concepts much easier to grasp. AI provides a more thorough and dependable analysis of complex data. However, it will still struggle to deliver an interpretation of unearthed patterns that may be easy to understand for humans.

*Gamification—*essentially putting the investor at the heart of the process, feeding suitable information and providing easy to understand and powerful interaction will play the largest role here. Yet, this requires human creativity and design that is currently not achievable by AIs.

Diversification—how easy is it to achieve a diverse investment? Diversification is a well-established corner stone of risk management. Ceteris paribus a diverse investment is more robust in times of change than a narrow investment. For now, the level of diversity in an investment is largely restricted by number of humans that can jointly pay attention to it (complexity of management). AI does not have this restriction and can therefore work on a much higher level of granularity than humans could reasonably do. Moreover, machines equipped with AI are also not bound by pre-established categories like industry sector and can come up with their own, purely based on the data at hand and the underlying correlations. As markets change structurally, this assessment can adapt seamlessly. Microtransactions and Smart Contracts will also allow for more tailored and suitable responses to changing market conditions. Rebalancing a portfolio becomes a more targeted process. Blockchain technology will allow for ad-hoc creation of alternative means to account for investments, possibly on a per-contract basis. The big enabler feeding all these developments will be Big Data. It provides a wide playing field for the aforementioned algorithms and technologies. Future investments will be much more diverse and also much quicker to change gears should the market require it.

Transaction costs—how low can they get? Transaction costs are falling. How fast are they falling and what drives this decrease? As more automated business models are established two patterns will emerge. A business can choose to keep the cost advantage, their margins will increase and the transaction price on the market will remain relatively unaffected. Alternatively, a business may choose to disrupt the market with significantly lower transaction costs. This sacrifices the potential for increased margins for an increase in market share and eventually increased revenue that outweighs the sacrificed margin. In reality, we will see both patterns overlap. Ultimately transaction costs will decrease further. The main technical enablers for this trend are Microtransactions and Smart Contracts. Although the main impact will be on transaction banks, the Wealth Management providers will also have to start embracing new, more cost-effective transaction services. Clients in the lower tier market segments are less likely to just accept traditional transaction costs on their smaller contract sizes. Furthermore, Wealth Management's value-based pricing (i.e. margin on assets under management) is acceptable, when there is a differentiation in value. If technology equalizes the value created, pricing will converge towards a (lower) margin on cost.

Minimal effective investment size—how small can it get? Directly influenced by the transaction costs is the minimum size of an investment that still economically makes sense (minimal effective size). However, there is more to the equation than just fees and commissions payable for an investment: the non-monetary transaction cost. With decreasing size, the number of investments and positions will increase. This leads to an increased overhead for monitoring, risk management and correcting of positions when needed. AI will take up much of this burden, supported by Big Data. Smart Contracts will allow machines to interpret contracts more accurately. With this decrease in ambiguity comes a decrease in operational risk and smaller contracts become feasible. This may even reach a point where multiple smaller contracts may be preferable to one large contract. For investments that are completely automated, the minimum effective investment size will drop to fractions of a cent. This drop will only be limited by the transaction cost incurred by energy, bandwidth and infrastructure. [2]

De-Centralization (Peer to Peer). The advantages of large, fully integrated providers will be offset gradually by their inability to change quickly enough to keep up with more agile FinTech ventures. It is unlikely, however, that their business will entirely dry up. Some of the more standardized transaction types where transaction costs are already very low are still best served by large scale ventures. Around these core providers we will see a multitude of services emerging. Many will only cover a specific segment of the value chain, such as advisory or custody while others will cater to certain segments of the product space. Their offerings will be viable in a new ecosystem of co-dependent services which—in its entirety—will provide equally seamless services as do the large, integrated providers. The enablers for this decentralized service landscape will come from Open APIs and Cloud Services. Smart contracts will also reduce the barriers for integration, as it is no longer a matter of opinion how a transaction is interpreted between different providers. As all necessary attributes and decision-making logic is codified in the Smart Contract, there is by definition only one common interpretation. There will be a strong evolutionary pressure among these smaller service providers. Many will disappear as quickly as they had surfaced, but some will become a part of a new strong framework that uses a decentralized service architecture. In addition, some of the more stable business models will be soon absorbed by the remaining large, fully integrated providers.

Entry barriers. As of 2018, still roughly half of the world's population does not have access to the Internet [1]. Moreover, for the majority of those who do have access, computer and financial literacy is still underdeveloped. In addition, even fewer are in the income ranges qualifying for wealth management services. So far, it has mostly been the High Net Worth Individuals (HNWIs) segment which enjoyed wealth management services. Yet, with the onset of WealthTech, serving affluent (and below) customer segments becomes economically feasible. Also, the demand for more bespoke services by these clients increases. On the other end of the wealth scale, very basic services for payments and micro loans were established in developing countries. Technology will eventually close the gap and will permit a coffee farmer to directly invest in commodity contracts, represented in a way so that he or she can truly comprehend what the investment is made in. Accessing the respective platforms is not the main challenge here but providing reliable and fair advisory to the financially barely literate. For this, gamification and microtransactions will pave the way.

Increased Investment Volatility. Throughout history technology has been an accelerator of progress, yet today the rate of change is bigger than ever before.

Clearly, there has been setbacks, when investments were getting detached from economic realities with the Dotcom and sub-prime bubble only being the latest examples. A loss of trust and increased regulation have throttled these fast-paced trends. Currently, the same is expected of the cryptocurrency frenzy. These setbacks have not stopped the acceleration, though, but merely brought it back to a speed where it is still manageable by humans and by the means of current of technology. With the increased capability of AIs to make quick, decisive changes to an investment portfolio or the competition of investment bots trying to outsmart each other we will undoubtedly also see increased levels of volatility in the market. Rather than constantly fluctuating wildly, we will see an increase in sharp, decisive corrections of the market. This pattern is similar to earthquakes in the overall context of continental drift. A positive side effect of tighter coupled financial markets could be that the corrections are getting more frequent, but perhaps less extreme. Even though it may be a long way before the collective intelligence of algorithms realizes that inflating a bubble and trying to get out of it in time is a highly risky proposition. But then, perhaps the risk/reward profile of these bubbles is convincing enough for them to become a permanent feature of our investment landscape.

Ubiquity of Asset Management. Wealth management today is an obvious affair. The wealth manager and the investor are acutely aware when they are engaging in wealth management activities. Yet, is this quality bound to persist? It does not seem likely. There will always be those clients that consciously want to engage in the investment process. But there will also be others which find the process tedious and intimidating. HNWIs can easily opt out by offloading more of the process to the wealth manager. Less affluent people cannot afford the cut this takes out of their investments and can only abstain from more interesting forms of investment. This will change as Gamification and enhanced user experience will make the process less dreary. AIs or rather personal investment assistants will also take over more and more tasks currently reserved for wealth managers. This will make the business of wealth managers more challenging to sustain, as even HNWIs are increasingly less likely to pay a steep service charge for tasks their mobile phone might offer for free. In the future you just grant Alexa, Cortana, Google Assistant or Siri access to your account, income and portfolio and they will talk you through investment decisions at your appropriate level. Subsequently they will execute them.

Client Profile—Shift from Client to Customer to User. The new WealthTech world will see a shift in the demographics of wealth management clients. Having said that, be aware that this sentence actually indicates two major shifts. First, asset management services will no longer be restricted to HNWIs. Instead, affluent and even low-income individuals will become investors, even though they may not actually call these services wealth management or even realize that they have assets under management.

Second, we will see a shift from 'Client' to 'Customer' to 'User'. The client base will break apart, diversifying their investments across multiple providers and services. As Clients become more agnostic towards who provides their services, they become Customers, who may change providers frequently.

When the decision for a provider or an investment is no longer intentional, but implicit, we have reached the final stage of this development. A consolidation where portals and applications allow users consolidated access to services and investment strategies. Wealth managers would not be talking to clients any more but rather offer services to users through an intermediate layer of technology.

CONCLUSION

The new world will be great for the consumers, the users of wealth management as it will be affordable at much lower income levels. The new world will also be great for companies providing aggregation services. Besides, it will be full of exciting make or break experiences for those providing specific services or investment opportunities. It will be hard on full-service wealth managers who pursue the strategy to capture all their client's business. Too much of their business model depends on their 'monopoly' to direct their client's investment decision. This will be very difficult to let go of this monopoly, until clients will eventually become users of systems where they feel more fairly treated. To prevail, these wealth managers should open to other services in the market, to provide their clients with a portal that presents competitors' investments, advisory agents and analysis capability on equal footing with their own. Naturally, the current big players will look for creative interpretations on how "equal" that footing is. They will compete with new players, though, which may first provide aggregation services and only secondly their own products or possibly not at all. To illustrate, think of Amazon how it began selling third party products, most notably books, and only lately offered their own products and services. Essentially, they provide a platform for other sellers. This is in stark contrast to other players such as Bertelsmann who have several distribution channels which are heavily biased towards their own products.

Eventually, we will see a landscape composed of successful new enterprises that do not source their revenues through a margin on the assets under management but by charging a margin on their cost. These would be either new FinTech ventures or established BigTech companies extending into WealthTech [3]. They may even provide free services to the user, getting their revenue through advertising or commissions for coupling services.

Then, there will be established players who manage to onboard third-party offerings in order to offer them to their clients. Clearly, in that case they would have to amend their pricing structures to stay competitive with their own products. They would potentially also absorb some of the more promising startups.

Lastly, there will be a few old school survivors whose dwindling competitive edge is a human interface and the trust advantage built over decades in the business. Their prices will remain steep, yet they will be increasingly challenged by their clients who will ask "Is it worth this much?". Additionally, their clientele which pay premium for the human interaction versus an AI supported App interface is decreasing in numbers. These players will see the most pressure for consolidation.

REFERENCES

1. https://en.wikipedia.org/wiki/Global_Internet_usage
2. The number of computations per joule of energy dissipated has been doubling approximately every 1.57 years. This trend has been remarkably stable since the 1950s. Increases in the number of computations-per-joule-of-energy-dissipated must come to a halt by about 2050: because the limit implied by Landauer's principle will be reached by then, according to Koomey's law.
3. According to the *World Wealth Report,* 56.2% of HNWI are open to BigTech companies serving their Wealth Management needs. Retrieved from: https://worldwealthreport.com/wp-content/uploads/sites/7/2019/07/World-Wealth-Report-2019-1.pdf

CHAPTER 6

THE PITFALLS OF INVESTING 4.0

Hendrik Emrich

This contribution deals with the pros and cons of digital investing. Special attention is paid to Robo-advisors and explaining the risks of excluding human experts from investment decisions processes. The author shows ways of digital matchmaking, explains why investors are unable to achieve their financial goals and why voice will be the next big thing in finance.

The global banking industry is currently undergoing tremendous change in all aspects of the value chain, be it payment, lending, saving or financial aggregation. Contributing to all this change is the pressure from fast-growing FinTech companies, open banking platforms and new application programming interfaces made possible by game-changing rules like the second payment service directive (PSD2), with the result that the traditional barriers between incumbents and smaller financial service providers are beginning to vanish. At the same time transaction costs are diminishing. Increasingly, traditional banking services can now be offered by small FinTech companies focusing on a particular market niche, thus making the famous quote attributed to Bill Gates, "banking is necessary, banks are not" becoming truer every day. At the same time, it has become common wisdom that the only real assets left for banks are the following two: They still have a significant customer base while at the same time they oversee large quantities of funds. When talking about co-operation between incumbent firms and FinTechs, for the latter one these two assets are the only things that truly matter. In banking, trust, confidence and reputation remain key. These attributes extend

WealthTech: Wealth and Asset Management in the FinTech Age, pages 35–38.

to asset management and advisory services. Innovations in this area are characterized by the rise of Robo-advisors. These new players offer a passive rule-based approach to investment. The fact is, this is not a new concept. For many years, asset managers have been applying passive, algorithm-based investment approaches in fund management. What is new is that this service can now be made available in a cost-efficient manner to small investors. So, if the innovation does not come from a new or disruptive investment style, what really explains the expansion of Robo-advisors? The answer is that the innovation these "new kids on the block" can offer lies in the purely digital touchpoints to their clients. Via the Internet personalized frontends, online marketing campaigns, and a seamless digital customer journey are enabling Robo-advisors to increasingly win over clients from traditional banks or wealth managers who cannot offer such a digital experience. Moreover, many Robo-advisors validate their "new" investment approach by citing behavioral finance experts and academic studies, which have concluded that active asset management does not offer any systematic yield pick-up to passive investment. While this might hold true for highly liquid large cap equity markets, this is usually not the case for smaller, less liquid markets. Here active asset management still makes a great deal of sense. In these less transparent market niches, good research and active fund management will always pay off. This was already proven by Eugene/Fama in the scope of their ground-breaking "Efficient Market theory" academic research paper.

However, Robo-advisory clients benefit from lower costs and an enhanced digital experience. Plus, clients no longer have to go to their bank to meet with their account manager. Instead, they are now able to execute banking transactions 24/7, wherever, whenever and from whatever device. In addition to performance, this freedom from having to physically travel to the bank is of great value for the Robo-advisory client. In a world of information overflow, offering a smart, clear and purely digital approach to asset management is highly appealing; however, this should never be valued higher than risk/return metrics and traditional asset management KPIs.

Due to the short track record of Robo-advisors (less than five years for most of the German players and in a positive market climate), it is too early to conclude whether machine or human performs better in asset allocation. At the end of the day, performance and risk parameters should tip the scale for B2C customers, most of whom are in desperate need for better financial advice and robust asset allocations. However, the ultimate problem is the investors' lack of understanding in and impatience with the stock markets. This combined with too often bad financial advice they may have received in the past, explains the underperformance of German investors in past decades.

THE PREFERENCE FOR DIGITAL RISK PROFILING VERSUS FACE-TO-FACE INTERVIEWS WITH A BANKER

When it comes to risk profiling and investment advice, clients are more and more turning to a digital approach. This may be due to the lack of willingness to share personal data and preferences when sitting face-to-face to a banker and/or a lack of understanding and trust in the banker's investment proposal. Recent studies show that clients still feel that their bank(er) is not able to adequately answer their questions and do not trust their investment decisions. These behavioral finance issues are the foremost obstacle: hindering clients from achieving their financial goals.

To address this, we decided to develop the "Portal 72" app to find out if gathering the investor's risk profile though a purely digital journey may lead to better results than traditional risk classification by face-to-face interviews.

The feedback from investors using our prototype has largely been positive, users appreciate a simple, smart and well-designed investment journey. Making risk-profiling more hands-on and visual with colorful interfaces creates a pleasant emotive experience. This emotive awareness is completely new concept in the investment process.

SURPRISING FINDINGS FROM DIGITAL MATCHMAKING APP

However, in the area of prototyping and investment proposals, we have found that there are parts in this "matchmaking process" where the assistance by human experts is still needed. As Figure 6.1 shows, we ask the user to intuitively decide which of the following three charts red (equity fund), green (balanced/mixed fund) or blue (time deposits) appealed to them the most. The results were striking with roughly a fifty-fifty photo-finish between red and green charts. No one of the several hundred users taking part, chose the blue chart.

FIGURE 6.1.

What is furthermore noticeable is that this result is in strong contradiction to the actual asset allocation of German investors, most of whom have their money invested in zero-interest money market funds, savings accounts and time deposits. Statistics show that less than 10% of the German population actually own shares. So why did this result occur?

This major finding of Portal 72 is strong evidence for the impact of behavioral finance, sometimes people will tell you one thing and then act completely differently. How can the Robo-advisor, full of comprehensive AI, machine learning and cutting-edge algorithms ever incorporate this? We believe this will never be possible, there will always be the need for human assistance.

We will ever need the support of smart managers adapting to different and highly diverse client needs. Active asset management should never become an "easy-to-get" commodity but remain a real "art" which is the result of hard work and dedication and deserves a reasonable price. At the same time, those financial advisors who are better able to explain to clients the pros and cons of taking on risk through equity investments will be seen as a valuable resource of our investment society.

THE PROMINENT ROLE OF VOICE IN DIGITAL INVESTING

As witnessed in other markets, there is a good probability that Voice will also be of value in finance. Not only could consumers execute their financial housekeeping through Alexa/Echo (i.e. transfer money, gather information about stock markets, making portfolio adjustments), but Voice could also play a major role in risk profiling. Assuming that both voice recognition and analytics technology will advance further, it might one day be possible to assess the clients' needs only by analyzing his voice.

It is not only important to analyze what is actually said but how it is said. Why should it not be possible to gain new insights into a person's hidden needs and preferences by analyzing his/her emotions, tonality and spirit when talking with a chatbot? Voice experts can collect data, gather information, and uncover needs the user himself or herself would never think of.

While people often say one thing and act the complete opposite, their digital footprint can also be ambiguous and misleading. However, people cannot disguise their voice. Expect to see many new FinTech ventures concentrating on voice analytics as a future disruptor of the banking sector. Voice-based risk profiling and asset management will also play a prominent role in overcoming the limitations of behavioral finance, supporting investors to better achieve their financial goals and making an important contribution to overall wealth and wellbeing.

PART 3

SOCIETAL TRENDS AFFECTING
WEALTH & ASSET MANAGEMENT

CHAPTER 7

DEMOCRATIZATION OF BANKING SERVICES IN EMERGING MARKETS: MEXICO

Felix Cardenas and Maurizio Ballesteros

Greater financial inclusion to the bottom of the pyramid population, and access to capital has provoked emerging markets including Asian, African, and Latin American countries to democratize FinTech. This section discussion the roots and implications of this trend in Mexico.

EMERGING MARKETS FINTECH

Nowadays, the amount of FinTech related investments in ASEAN has jumped 45% to USD 366m in 2017 compared to USD 252m in 2016.[1] In emerging markets, it is particularly, interesting to observe the strong correlation between mobile-based innovation and FinTech market absorption, for example, already today more than half of the population across emerging and developing countries such as Mexico, Venezuela, Colombia, South Africa, Kenya, India, Vietnam, Philippines, Tunisia, Jordan, Lebanon have access to smart phones. The adoption of smartphone is driven by demographics of a growing middle class[2].

---

[1] E&Y, ASEAN *Fintech Census 2018.* Retrieved from: https://www.ey.com/Publication/vwLUAssets/EY-asean-fintech-census-2018/$FILE/EY-asean-fintech-census-2018.pdf
[2] Pew Global Research, *Mobile connectivity in emerging economies, 2019.* Retrieved from: https://www.pewinternet.org/2019/03/07/mobile-connectivity-in-emerging-economies/#fn-22186-1

WealthTech: Wealth and Asset Management in the FinTech Age, pages 41–46.

In Africa, smartphones have been a key component promoting financial inclusion. Smartphones have provided access and widened FinTech applications. For example, in Kenya's M-PESA allows money transfer and in Tanzania, a mobile phone system has been used for initial public offering subscriptions which led to doubling investors subscription.

In Mexico the recent increase in the use of smartphones represents a technology access of these devices. In 2012, the average retail price of a smartphone in Mexico was USD 318, representing about 40% of the monthly average income. By 2014 the average price was reduced to USD 185 accruing to 20% of the monthly income. This increased affordability as well as the constitutional reform to the Law of Telecommunications in 2014[3], created the emergence of more supply providers competing in the market. For instance, in terms of mobile data, in 2015 AT&T started offering its services and promoted further competition[4].

MEXICO AN EMERGING MARKET

Mexico is the largest Spanish-speaking market in Latin America with 126 million[5] inhabitants. Mexico is Latin America's second largest economy with a USD 122tr. GDP, placing it as the 15th largest economy in the world, and in terms of exports the 11th largest worldwide. Mexico has not only implemented structural reforms encouraging competition and investments, but Mexico, is also finding opportunities in the banking and financial services sectors. Loan penetration in Mexico currently stands among the lowest in all of Latin America, hence innovative financial service providers have started to position themselves along with leading FinTech trends on the forefront of a growing service industry. Reforms in areas including telecommunications, economic competition, financial services and labor markets have provided legal certainty which has increased foreign investment in Mexico.

Mexico is a key player in emerging markets for IT and FinTech. The structural reforms are resulting in strong demands for IT infrastructure, creating more opportunities for suppliers of technology and IT services. This reflects the increasing importance of the region in the world economy and in the IT industry, where Mexico and Brazil are key players within Latin-American emerging markets.

SOCIETAL TRENDS: PEER-TO-PEER
LENDING TECH AND REMITTANCES

Lending tech includes primarily peer-to-peer (P2P) lending platforms using machine learning technologies and algorithms to measure creditworthiness. While, money transfer/remittance encompass P2P platforms to transfer money between

---

[3] Instituto Federal de Telecomunicaciones."Reforma constitucional", 2016.http://www.ift.org.mx/que-es-el-ift/reforma-constitucional#

[4] Paulina Santibáñez. "¿Cuál es el panorama del sector FinTech?". Entrepreneur, September 25, 2015. https://www.entrepreneur.com/article/268987

[5] World Bank, *Data for 2018,*, https://data.worldbank.org/country/mexico

individuals across countries. P2P lending and remittances have been the fastest growing FinTech areas in emerging markets. These address the market need to finance SMEs. The estimated credit lending gap for the formal small and medium sized enterprise (SME) sector in emerging markets has been estimated to be USD 1.2tr., while the total credit gap for both formal and informal SMEs is approximately USD 2.6tr. In Mexico credit for SME business, represents 95% of businesses accruing to four million SMEs[6], of which 30% use some information technology. 37% of Mexicans have access to formal financial services[7].

Remittances are a very important contribution to Mexican national development. According to Mexico's central bank, in 2016 between January and November USD 24.6bn were send to Mexico from friends and family members living overseas, most of which originated in USA. Remittances in Mexico are higher than oil exports, remittances provide support to Mexico's economy, ranging from new home to school construction.

SOCIAL EFFECTS ON FINTECH BANKING SERVICES SUPPLY AND DEMAND

After the 2008 financial meltdown, there was a generalized mistrust from consumers towards established financial institutions. Consumers demanded more transparent services[8]. Entrepreneurs, often millennials with a stronger affinity to technology were also among those dissatisfied customers. These entrepreneurs started to offer solutions by making technology accessible and deciding to use technology to go around an aging established banking financial system characterized by hundreds of intermediaries[9]. Startups commenced providing innovative user experiences. This development also took place in Mexico, where 61% of the Mexican adult population still lacks access to financial services[10]. The members of this underserved population do not have a bank account, and this represents a serious opportunity to improve the quality of life and alleviate poverty[11].

There is a lack of investment culture and education in Mexico at several socioeconomic levels. There is a clear set of needs to be met in the Mexican market, however the introduction of financial services to solve these business opportunities is not enough. Even though it may seem as a huge untapped market and busi-

---

[6] Instituto Nacional de Estadística y Geografía (INEGI), http://en.www.inegi.org.mx/programas/eac/2010/

[7] Global Findex 2017 database, World Bank, https://globalfindex.worldbank.org/

[8] Myers. "FinTech's 'Third Wave' is coming, and it will change everything". Forbes. October 3, 2016.

[9] FinTech Radar México: México se convierte en el mayor mercado FinTech de América Latina". Finnovista: agosto, 30 2016. http://www.finnovista.com/FinTech-radar-mexico/

[10] Amanda Jacobson. "Mexico's 3 greatest financial inclusion challenges, as defined by 20 experts." December 2, 2015. https://medium.com/village-capital/mexico-s-3-greatest-financial-inclusion-challenges-asdefined-by-20-experts-cb37952ff0fc#.rsvfjh1g

[11] ¿Qué es la Inclusión Financiera?" Asociación Mexicana de Sociedades Financieras Populares (AMSOFIPO). http://www.amsofipo.mx/inclusion.html

ness opportunity, if the culture or education is not embedded in its potential market, as intuitive and comprehensive this tool may be, the market may not yet be ready for it. This certainly applies to wealth and asset management in Mexico. In addition to the asset management services offered by banks, there are other financial institutions, such as brokerage houses and asset managers that offer wealth management. However, these organizations cater their services only to the top 1% of the country.

This in turn opens a door to start innovation in other financial services, such as fully digital banks, characterized by fast and reliable loan processing, payment methods and value-added services that help keep track of transactions and company operations. According to the FinTech Radar Mexico created by Finnovista in 2016, the largest share of FinTech startups is focused on Payments with a total of 30%, followed by Lending with 32% of total FinTech startups focusing on this type of service. The bottom segments are Trading and Markets with 2%, Wealth Management, Scoring, Identity & Fraud, and Personal Financial Management with 3% each. This gives us a clear picture of the tendencies and services in demand in the Mexican market.

At the present moment, there is a handful of successful growing FinTech startups in Mexico, such as Konfio, Kueski, Kubo Financiero and Clip, among others. According to Expansion business magazine, these four raised a third of the total investment in startups in Mexico in 2016. The first three of them are focused on lending and Clip is a payment platform. Even though currently there is a limited number of startups in a later stage that show impressive growth, these types of cases should multiply in the coming years. While these cases have so far been predominantly for the lending and payments side, it is to be expected that also more WealthTech firms will emerge once the market matures.

BanRegio, a regional bank based in Monterrey, Mexico, is looking at the tech startup sector with two main objectives in mind. One of them is to cater these startups and entrepreneurs. This sector is underserved and there is a very small number of financial products available for them due to their lean structure and aggressive scalability roadmap. This Mexican bank is looking to reengineer some of its products such as bank accounts and business credit cards and develop new ones such as venture debt, user account creation and funding that are suitable for this segment. This will be of great support for the ecosystem and its growth. The second objective the bank will achieve is to attract innovation through FinTech startups. Working closely with them will help develop new services for the BanRegio's current clients that will enhance their user experience and help them grow their businesses. In order to do this, BanRegio has engaged in investing in venture capital funds as well as FinTech startups at an early stage to become a key ally for their growth. These types of involvements from established banks are factors that were not present earlier in Mexico that with no doubt will impulse the creation of new startups and revolutionize financial services as we know them. In terms of growth and traction from startups we see Konfio's success, led by founder and

CEO David Arana. 95% of business in Mexico fall under the SME category and are in need of finance for growth. This social and economic condition among owners of SMEs needs disruptive innovation. Konfio's take on this problem has proved to be a service that adds value to the customer.

Additionally, in terms of social behaviors being key to develop a winning Fin-Tech service. Startups learn why consumer demographics favor certain product or service. More than 50% of Mexico's population is under 30 years of age and as mentioned earlier mobile penetration is growing in Mexico. These Millennial and Gen Z's have a different way of looking at technology. They are much more open to usage of platforms to obtain products and services, including financial services. One important factor to take into consideration though, is their social behavior that directly affects what kind of services and products they use. Let us not forget that millennials are perceived to be more selfish than other generations, often-times value experiences over goods, typically forego higher salaries for better working environments, leave home and marry at a later stage, often have higher levels of consciousness, among other interesting mindsets and behaviors. In addition, we need to factor in culture and education. An example to how there is a product-market gap is banks catering to millennial. Many young entrepreneurs and individuals do not like to interact with banks because of what they perceive as an extremely deficient user experience. Millennials are used to getting things done almost instantly and multiple layers of formalities and complex processes are seen as roadblocks to this efficiency, which in turn drives people away from these incumbent institutions. Banks must revolutionize the way they serve people in order to survive. Some banks are betting on fully digital services, other on personalized but efficient services. Chatbots, branchless operations, Artificial Intelligence (AI) operated electronic banking are some examples of efforts to improve the way people do banking, but there is still a long way to go.

Separately, Wealth and Asset Management in Mexico is a financial service that has yet to be addressed. Asset management communication is still extremely technical and can be deciphered by a few. Besides creating a friendlier interaction with users, a key value to factor in is trust. People are still risk averse and distrust wealth managers, let alone fully digital companies that offer to manage one's life's work. Democratizing these wealth and asset management services is also a challenge for the sector. The Mexican wealth and asset management industry must do away with the perception that one needs to be a high net-worth individual to have access to capital markets, real estate or investment opportunities. This notion must fade away and neophytes must be allowed in the market. However, the challenge does not lie only in opening these barriers but educating the relevant population segments on the benefits and ample options of wealth and asset management.

Compared to wealth and asset management FinTech lending is already making its breakthrough in Mexico. For years, retail and company lending has been through banks or usurers and almost all the time require collateral in order to get the loan. This in turn limited the market to those who had something to get loans on. FinTech is paving the way to new, better and more efficient ways of lending in order to serve a previously underserved market. Kueski and Konfio are both startups that offer loans in an easy and intuitive way. Kueski offers loans to individuals in as little as 30 minutes using algorithms to assess risk. As previously mentioned, Konfio offers loans to SMEs. Both of these companies have a fully digital credit application process, offer a very fast response to their clients and do not require collateral for their loans. We hope that some WealthTech firms will follow suit soon.

RESOURCES

Andrade, G., Fontao, A., Pombo, C., Morelos, E., Pleguezelos, J., & Goulart, J. (2017, May). *FINTECH: Innovations you may not know were from Latin America and the Caribbean* (pp. 77–80). Inter-American Development Bank and Finnovista.

CBInsights. (2019, July). *Global Fintech report Q2 2019.* Retrieved from: https://www.cbinsights.com/research/report/fintech-trends-q2-2019/

Cuesta, H., & Cardier, L. (2017, March). Emerging markets—Opportunities and risk management. *Financier Worldwide Magazine.* Retrieved from: https://www.financierworldwide.com/special-report-emerging-markets-opportunities-and-risk-management#. XXCLhCgzaUk

Dib, D., Ramírez, J., & Alvarado, G. (2017, February). *Panorama del FinTech en Mexico.* Mexico City, NM: Fiinlab Endeavor. Retrieved from: http://www.crowdfunding-mexico.mx/uploads/8/7/7/2/87720184/panorama_fintech_mexico.pdf,

IOSCO. (2017, February). *Research Report on Financial Technologies.* FinTech. Retrieved from: https://www.iosco.org/library/pubdocs/pdf/IOSCOPD554.pdf

Ramos, R. (2016, March). Market analysis: Mexico leads the pack among emerging markets. *The National.* Retrieved from: https://www.thenational.ae/business/markets/market-analysis-mexico-leads-the-pack-among-emerging-markets-1.156302

CHAPTER 8

WHY BITCOIN IS NOT A CURRENCY BUT A SPECULATIVE REAL ASSET

Dietmar Peetz and Gregory Mall

Bitcoin's price has seen a meteoric rise over the last years. We hold that Bitcoin is a real asset but what is not real is the value assigned to it. We argue that Bitcoin has reached bubble territory and will ultimately correct. However, we believe that in the intermediate term, the bubble can become even bigger in the process of financialization. It is to bear in mind that Bitcoin is not for the faint hearted but for speculative investors with very high-risk tolerance.

INTRODUCTION

In 2019, digital currencies have been a hot topic. Bitcoin, the now dominant representative of the crypto currency industry, has seen further dramatic price increases. From 2009, the year of introduction, until end of August 2019, Bitcoin's rise has been super-exponential, just recently surpassing a market cap of more than USD 190bn. Despite all the media hype, we contend in this article that Bitcoin, like all other crypto currencies, should not be seen as a currency in terms of a medium of exchange, but rather as a distinct asset class. Nevertheless, given crypto currencies' meteoric price increases, we believe the crypto currency sphere to be in

WealthTech: Wealth and Asset Management in the FinTech Age, pages 47–55.

bubble territory, making eventual consolidation inevitable. In this sense, investors may be well served to recall that asset valuations go from boom to bust—from overvaluation to undervaluation (and eventually back to overvaluation). As a result, we believe that Bitcoin, as it is currently valued (September 5, 2019) juxtaposed against monetization reality and ill-defined monetization (profit) prospects, is a speculation, not an investment. Accordingly, speculators with very high risk (volatility) tolerance may find "cryptos" of interest.

WHAT IS BITCOIN?

Bitcoin is based on a public ledger system—a so-called blockchain, where all transactions made in Bitcoins are recorded in a cryptographic and hence anonymous manner. Every time a Bitcoin is transacted from one digital wallet to another, it will be documented on the blockchain. A person owning Bitcoins holds a unique digital key to access his/her Bitcoins. Whoever owns the key, controls the Bitcoins. If the key is lost, the Bitcoins are lost. Transactions are irreversible, and settlement occurs as soon as the ledger is updated. Updating the blockchain ensues by solving a computationally intensive mathematical puzzle. The computer (node) that solves this puzzle first and contributes to the blockchain receives a certain number of Bitcoins (so-called "mining," a purposeful analogy to labor and energy intensive precious metals mining). The number of awarded Bitcoins will subsequently be halved every four years after that. The total amount of Bitcoins is fixed at 21 million. The blockchain is distributed among all nodes and can only be manipulated if any one-party controls over 50% of the computing power.

WHY BITCOIN IS NOT A TRANSACTION CURRENCY

The original idea of Bitcoin was to create a purely anonymous peer-to-peer payment system based on cryptographic proof rather than on a trusted third-party intermediary. Because of its de-centralized nature, the idea quickly gained traction in the libertarian as well as countercultural movement. Many saw it as the manifestation of ideas nurtured in the Austrian School of Economics. Specifically, a currency liberated from any sort of governmental interference, which would facilitate true price discovery, the backbone of robust, free market capitalism. This was also the reason why Bitcoin became popular on the Dark Net, enabling safe and anonymous transactions with no interference of traditional financial intermediaries. But is Bitcoin truly a currency? Let us analyze the facts:

A currency is an instrument which is used to facilitate transactions between parties. It is a medium of exchange meant to help buyers and sellers to find the right price at which a transaction can take place. It is at this price that economics says the market has "cleared." Clearing is important because it helps to bring transparency and predictability to the marketplace, which in turn strengthens social reciprocity and encourages more transactions. However, when a currency cannot be accurately valued, this clearing mechanism does not work anymore

(Weimar hyperinflation being the classic example). That is the point when behaviors become irrational, such as aggressive bidding for fear of more currency in circulation (inflation) or refusing to use the currency in anticipation of less currency in circulation (deflation). In view of Bitcoin being labeled a currency, suffice it to say that we see several reasons speaking against Bitcoin having currency-like characteristics. First, there currently exists no commonly accepted valuation model for Bitcoin. Second, unlike precious metals, highly volatile Bitcoin has no history of being accepted as money and it lacks any time-tested store of value credentials (accepted intrinsic worth), both of which are key currency attributes. Third, all else being equal, Bitcoin would have potentially material deflationary consequences. Digital production is programmed to stop when the total number of Bitcoins reaches 21m (17.9m have been "mined" already). If Bitcoin had to be used to facilitate all transactions in the world, that would lead to a contracting world economy very similar to the austerity policies imposed on Greece, but on a much larger (global) scale. In contrast, consider that central banks have the mandate not only to ensure the stability of the financial system, but also to manage their respective nations' fiat money supplies with the objective to achieving inter alia price stability, i.e., to prevent either excessive inflation or deflation. Fourth, we are of the opinion that the same fears of deflation, which were used as a rationale for the US to abandon the Gold standard in 1971, would embolden authorities to prevent Bitcoin from becoming a currency.[1] Based on historical precedents, it is not unthinkable that in times of economic or financial crisis, political and regulatory pressure on an unwanted currency would increase, possibly in a similar manner as in the US in 1934, when the Gold Reserve Act of 1934 was ratified, nationalizing all gold and subsequently revaluing it by 69% in US dollar terms.

The finite limit of Bitcoins has additional drawbacks. The majority of coins are expected to be "mined" in the next 20 years which, in the absence of a large-scale hardware revolution, will lower the individual incentive for "miners" to perform the computationally intensive settlement process. Although—due to the generous "mining" system—Bitcoin transactions and the energy to "mine" Bitcoins are currently cheap for the individual buyer and seller, the process itself is excessively energy intensive. Currently, Bitcoin's aggregate energy consumption is estimated to be around 66.7 Terra Watt/h per year (180 Kw/h per transaction), although there are only roughly 25 million people using Bitcoin[2]. "Mining" becomes more profitable the higher Bitcoin prices rise. That said, "miners" have to invest heavily into technology to keep pace with other "miners." When all Bitcoins have been minded the "miners" will then need to be compensated solely by transaction fees

---

[1] The basic relationship between money supply in circulation and value of aggregate transactions is shown in the famous quantity theory of money. For a good discussion Genreith 2014), "Field Theory of macroeconomics", https://arxiv.org/abs/1407.6334
[2] https://www.bitcoinmarketjournal.com/how-many-people-use-bitcoin/

which are unlikely to be lower than current transaction fees.[3] Based on generous estimates, Bitcoin can currently handle around 7 transactions per second[4]. Its rival Visa can currently handle around 65,000 transactions per second. Transaction capacity will depend on the opportunities provided by future hardware, but without radically scaling (huge, unearthed economies of scale), it is unlikely for Bitcoin to come anywhere near established payment systems. While increasingly more vendors will accept Bitcoins, we believe this is happening mostly for marketing purposes and this trend is most likely to reverse once the Bitcoin price enters bear market territory. In a related and most germane manner, the enormously high Bitcoin price volatility renders Bitcoin unsuitable for a reliable day-to-day exchange medium.

There are other reasons to be skeptical about the long-term prospects of Bitcoin as a currency. Apart from the obvious risks such as fraud, hacking, and theft, Bitcoin and other crypto currencies face a variety of legal hurdles to master. Due to its anonymity as well as its lack of governmental control, regulators around the world are not pleased with the relatively wide-spread acceptance Bitcoin has gained over the years. Since Bitcoins are regularly used to circumvent capital controls as well as potentially violate existing capital market statutes, it is possible that regulatory agencies may prohibit the possession of Bitcoins. The People's Bank of China has recently taken the strictest approach to date, declaring ICOs (initial coin offerings) as illegal[5]. The SEC has also started to scrutinize ICO-markets more closely, although the agency has not been as determined in its attempt to restrict the ICO process altogether. Other regulators around the globe are likely to follow suit. The bottom line is, however, that cryptos and ICOs will eventually be subject to the same compliance requirements as other capital and currency markets. This is likely dent both the appeal and the valuation of crypto currencies, possibly to substantial extent.

Even if governments do not explicitly regulate the exchange of Bitcoin, it is unlikely that they will accept it as a payment solution for levied taxes. Any individual person using only Bitcoin would still need to convert it into local currency in order to pay local taxes. The other issue emerges from the fact that Bitcoin is a purely virtual (cyberspace) asset/claim. Hence, select judicial branches of national governments have determined that Bitcoin should be viewed as property—not for legal protection, but for taxation reasons. Unlike other financial claims, with Bitcoin there is no counterparty involved. Therefore, there is no counterparty risk

---

[3] Scaling by increasing the current block size is a very controversial topic since the larger bitcoin community argues that this would defy Bitcoin's decentralized structure, the original raison d'être for the currency. It is interesting to note that 97% of all miners decided not to support Bitcoin cash but rather the current solution, a solution that some argue favors Bitcoin as an investment vehicle vs. a transactional currency.

[4]   https://steemit.com/cryptocurrency/@cryptocentral/bitcoin-segwit-ethereum-dash-and-ripple-vs-visa-and-paypal-transactions-per-second

[5]   https://www.bloomberg.com/news/articles/2017-09-04/china-central-bank-says-initial-coin-offerings-are-illegal

and no need for a credit risk premium. However, there have been reports of cases wherein owners which converted Bitcoins into cash had to wait several days, exposing the Bitcoin holders to liquidity risk and potentially price risk. We suspect that in the case of a Bitcoin bear market, more leveraged retail investors will try locking in gains, further contributing to the liquidity backlog problem. At such a stage, we would expect the market to start fully pricing in liquidity and price risks, which is likely to further drag down Bitcoin prices in a classical feedback loop.

WHY BITCOIN CREATED A NEW ASSET CLASS

On the surface, it is difficult to imagine how capital flows from Bitcoin can be routed into productive real economy investments such as building new factories or machinery—which return a profit including a risk premium to the capital owner. Cash flows and risk premiums are the main determinants to price traditional asset classes such as equities or bonds. Unfortunately, there exist currently no generally accepted financial model for pricing Bitcoin. Another technical problem would be that interest rates on loans made in Bitcoin would have to come from the limited money supply of Bitcoin itself, which further exacerbates the deflationary effects of Bitcoin.[6]

Humans have always been very creative in overcoming seemingly impossible problems, such as the ones of pricing Bitcoin. One possible solution is financialization, in which tangible or intangible capital or activities are transformed into financial instruments. We believe that financialization will transform Bitcoin into a distinct asset class. If Bitcoin can provide the means for broader investor participation—be it through vehicles such as exchange traded funds (ETF), funds, certificates, or derivatives—it could turn into a distinct asset class.

It is important to note that so far, it was predominantly retail investors and capital flows from China and other countries that drove the price of Bitcoin. Now that large financial institutions have initiated research coverage, other institutions are likely to follow suit. Acknowledging Bitcoins' current excessive price volatility, we agree with most analysts that its volatility will decrease once it becomes fully embedded into the financial system. Indeed, Bitcoin's volatility has been trending down since it reached peak levels in 2014, while its daily trading liquidity has shown an upward trend. The decline of volatility could further increase the attention of institutional investors, who are desperate for Beta-diversifying alternative investments in today's ultra-low or even negative yield environment. With increasing demand, financial innovation will ensure that new investment vehicles will emerge which, at a later stage, will be designed for leveraged speculators. A further milestone for the general acceptance of Bitcoin as a financial asset class could also be financialization. If a mechanism is created to use Bitcoin as collateral for debt financing in a traditional fiat currency setting, the asset class Bitcoin

---

[6] In addition, Bitcoin would need to become a construction of double entry accounting very similar to the rest of our monetary and financial system.

will be in even greater demand. Today, Bitcoin shows almost zero correlation to other major asset classes. As institutional investors add the financialized version of Bitcoin as a diversifier in a balanced portfolio, we expect its covariance properties to be similar to those of gold in the past.

Now, could Bitcoin become a new store of value function, similarly to physical gold? One of the main reasons for gold's success was its limited supply as well as its essentially perpetual shelf life. Bitcoin has no intrinsic value[7], but a utility value in addition to the described beneficial diversification properties. These characteristics add value from a portfolio management perspective. Furthermore, Bitcoin is more mobile but less fungible than physical gold. Bitcoin requires a technical network and energy input to exist. If the Bitcoin network loses a critical mass of computational power, it becomes utterly unusable. It can therefore be seen as a store of value within but not outside of its network. Interestingly, Bitcoin usage has seen its steepest increase in countries which are experiencing currency troubles such as India and Venezuela. Surbitcoin, Venezuela's largest bitcoin exchange saw accounts to skyrocket from 450 in 2014 to almost 100,000 in 2016.

WHY WE BELIEVE BITCOIN IS A BUBBLE AND WHY IT COULD CONTINUE FOR YEARS

Essentially, Bitcoin is software and needs energy to exist. We therefore argue that it is a real asset.[8] However, countless other enterprises, as capitalized during past manias, consumed prodigious amounts of energy and invested massively, yet never ended up reaching profitability or managed to attain earnings anywhere near the levels necessary to justify their previous bubble valuations or market caps. Those enterprises also comprised real assets. Correspondingly, what is not real—or perhaps 'rational' would be a better adjective—is Bitcoin's "value" when measured in a fiat currency terms such as USD. Some skeptics even go so far as to say that since the financial basis of Bitcoin is a fiat Ponzi scheme, Bitcoin's technology is only the masking shell of this Ponzi scheme.[9]

Since September 2015, the crypto currency has been in a long-term uptrend with momentum massively accelerating since July 2017. Although it is obvious that this price increase seems unsustainable in the long-term, there are arguments for a continuation of this trend for a foreseeable period of time.

A clear bubble indicator for Bitcoin as well as other crypto currencies seems to be the booming ICO (initial coin offering) market. The ICO market can be seen as a mix between seed investing and crowdfunding, in essence circumventing existing capital market regulations. There are thousands of startup companies,

---

[7] Fiat money has value by convention but isn't backed by any physical wealth.

[8] See Soddy (1926), "Wealth, Virtual Wealth and Debt", for a good definition of real assets.

[9] See Genreith, H. (2017), "Is the financial system a slow-motion Ponzi scheme?" http://genreith.de/ Genreith-Is-the-financial-system-a-slow-motion-Ponzi-scheme-JSB-Vol7No1April2017pp33-53. pdf

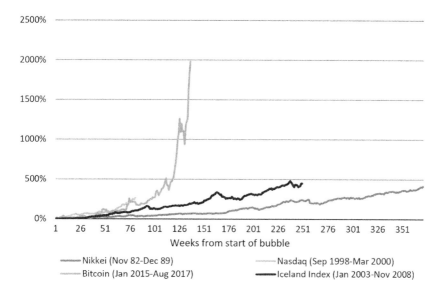

FIGURE 8.1.   Historical Performance in Not Indicative for Future Performance.
Source: own calculations

raising funds within seconds by issuing crypto currencies. Many of them see ICOs as cheap lottery tickets very similar to the IPO frenzy during the New Economy Hype beginning of the 2000s.

These coins and tokens often trade at penny-stock prices, experiencing dramatic price increases within hours and are often trading at very low liquidity. Most of these companies merely offer a so-called "white-papers" basically a business plan that explains which product a company wants to develop in the future and how it wants to market it. Most of these promised projects are praised as having huge potential but are extremely uncertain to be actually succeed. Since these ICOs are typically conducted in such a way that investors are obliged to pay with a crypto currency of one type or another, there is an inherent conflict of interest when it comes to converting crypto currencies into fiat currency. As long as the price is rising, most companies will probably only redeem the absolute minimum of their crypto-reserves for fiat currency—ironically also known as "hard cash"—in order to pay for overhead costs. Once the price falls, however, it is very likely that most of the Crypto-based companies will want to convert their reserves which may spark a chain reaction. Although the total market cap of ICO-companies is currently around USD 270bn, it is likely to grow further. In what may be viewed as a contrarian and bullish sign, funds raised through ICOs increased since the US securities and exchange commission began to caution investors[10]. We believe that

---

[10]   https://www.nytimes.com/2017/08/07/business/dealbook/initial-coin-offerings-sec-virtual-currency.html?ref=dealbook

if the ICO-market becomes big enough, the non-correlation between crypto currencies and equity markets might actually break down, i.e., the two asset classes become positively correlated. Although since its 2009 creation Bitcoin has shown a very low correlation to equity markets, it is worth remembering that this has been an exceptionally robust bull-market era. If equity markets would crash, other risk-off sentiment may potentially spillover to the ICO market and as a consequence to the crypto market.

It is also important to bear in mind that although ICO and the dotcom era are founded on irrational exuberance, at least the companies promised some sort of future cash flows. Cisco for example was a real company selling goods and recording cash flows. Crypto coins on the other hand—similarly to the tulip mania—do not generate value. In other words, as an investor it only makes sense to invest in crypto currencies due to the positive price trend. Since there is no intrinsic value, skeptics argue that in the long term the asset class has to fall back to the value of zero. Most investors acknowledge the bubble situation. However, they argue that central bank's easy money will help the bubble mania to grow even bigger, thus attracting even more investors (speculators) looking for easy profits. They remain bullish because of the Greater Fool Theory.

CONCLUSION

Bitcoin has become the flagship for an increasingly opaque crypto currency market. For the above-mentioned reasons and assuming that the currency is not being banned by major regulatory agencies, we believe the most realistic scenario for Bitcoin is one in which Bitcoin will continue to rise in price in the short to medium term. We furthermore expect to see an increased institutional demand prior to the initial hype fading away. At that juncture, Bitcoin's monetization or return prospect realities will begin to set in and, if history is any guide, eventually dominate valuation. Although we believe Bitcoin to be partially a bubble, this does not mean that the underlying blockchain-technology will not have a bright future in a financial as well as in a commercial context. The Blockchain will be a disruptive force in the long run and completely transform our financial system, similarly to the way stock ownership did in the 17th century. But as noted by Bloomberg columnist Matt Levine, there might be a long road ahead: "The first like 300 years of the history of stocks were filled with hucksters and hype and bubbles and disaster. Crypto currencies and blockchain really could be revolutionary technologies that will ultimately pervade every aspect of the economy, even while almost every individual project could be nonsense."[11] Just because the dotcom hype was a clear bubble, this does not mean that the Internet itself was not a groundbreaking technology. As is often the case with bubbles, fantasies are starting to go wild. No differentiation between sensible and irrational projects are made in those situa-

---

[11] https://www.bloomberg.com/view/articles/2017-08-23/blockchain-mania-and-mifid-ii

tions. While the immediate expectations are overblown, the long-term effects can still be disruptive.

A continuation of the Bitcoin frenzy similar to other speculative bubbles is possible with exactly the same long-term consequences. The trend of financialization will continue and ultimately overshadow the original idea of a digital payment system. Financialization of Bitcoin is neither bad nor good per se, but merely the symptom of a larger disease of a bubble building in investable monies and too few investments being made in the productive real economy, most notably in developed markets. Borrowing money for free and having easy access to capital and leverage (for big entities) is the fuel asset bubbles thrive on. By aggressively mitigating the effects of the 2008 financial crisis via unparalleled global monetary debasement extending for nearly a decade, central banks have brought us today's "bubbles everywhere" investment landscape. Once capital is not productive, it becomes destructive. From a historical perspective, valuations in traditional asset classes such as bonds as well as equities have become stretched. What is more, alternative investments often do not live up to their promises in terms of being a true beta diversifier. As a consequence, investors are looking for alternatives which they may have found in crypto currencies. But as in the Dutch tulip mania, investors (speculators) have to ask themselves: Where does any particular asset, such as Bitcoin, derive its value from? Bitcoin is not a financial asset in itself, it is a real asset, such as software or the Internet itself, and thus the law of entropy applies. Sustained growth in Blockchain usage is not viable unless affordable and abundant 24/7 energy is available—our strategic trajectory here is not cheery. In addition, Bitcoin cannot exist outside the social and financial system. Due to this inherent, inevitable integration, we expect the correlation to other asset classes, whether positive or negative, to increase in times of crises. A diversifier, after all, or just a big bubble looking for a pin?

CHAPTER 9

MILLENNIALS: THE NEW GENERATION OF WEALTH MANAGEMENT CLIENTS

David Gyori

Millennials are people becoming adults in the new millennium, i.e. in and after the year 2000. They are quickly evolving into the most valuable client segment globally, overtaking their parents: the Baby Boomers. Millennials have distinct wealth and asset management preferences. They demand instant, visual, community and social media centered, fully digital customer journeys. The question is: How to provide it to them?

According to US Census Bureau data, Millennials will be in a 'Position of Peak Profitability' between 2022 and 2055. This means that in the United States this generation will be the largest profit contributor for the business sector during this period. In other demographically younger regions, such as Africa and Asia, Millennials have already become the primary sources of corporate profit.

Who are the Millennials and why are they called so? Millennials are people being born in and after 1982. This makes them people who have or will become adults in the 'current millennium'.

Why is there so much attention focusing on the needs of this generation? Large corporations across industries and continents have focused over the past decades

WealthTech: Wealth and Asset Management in the FinTech Age, pages 57–62.
Copyright © 2020 by Information Age Publishing

on the needs of the Baby Boomers. Baby Boomers, the name given to the Post World War II baby boom, are the parents of the Millennials, and have contributed to the periods of peak profitability for past decades across the world. In most large corporations, marketing channels, customer communication, pricing, product development, segmentation and positioning are still explicitly or implicitly focused on the Baby Boomers, This has to change in order for incumbents across traditional industries, including banking, insurance, wealth management and asset management, to remain relevant and profitable in the decades ahead of us.

In this section, we will take a look at the six common names which the Millennials are often referred to and highlight the behavioral characteristics behind these names. Finally, we will define simple but practical ways wealth management and asset management companies can capitalize on these key qualities of the generation dominating the next three to four decades.

THE INSTANT GENERATION

Baby Boomers are often quoted saying: 'I only have five minutes'. The same sentence for Millennials is: 'I only have five seconds'. Millennials are used to the immediacy of services which largely is a result of the online world. Yet, corporations have maintained a traditional way of doing business requiring more time and effort to deliver and obtain products and services. This is an approach which Millennials widely reject. A good example for immediacy in financial services which Millennials appreciate is 'social media credit scoring'. Social media credit scoring is a new way of credit risk assessment by companies like Friendly Score, Big Data Scoring, Lenddo, HelloSoda, Sesame Credit and TALA. Users log into the website of the social media credit scoring company and share their browser history, Facebook activity, Tweets, LinkedIn profile, Instagram and Pinterest presence and immediately receive a social media credit score. Some companies focus on smart phone-based credit scores extracting, with permission of the user, a great depth of data from the smartphone. These big data techniques are common among users accessing P2P lending sites and requesting a loan online. The social media credit score is often the cornerstone of due diligence in online lending sites. Rather than the current processes which are time consuming and often paper intensive, the Millennial generation seeks solutions which are immediate.

THE GAFA GENERATION

GAFA stands for Google, Apple, Facebook and Amazon—the US technology giants. In Asia the same expression is referred to as 'The BAT Generation' referring to BaiDu, Alibaba and Tencent—the Chinese technology giants. Millennials are more confident doing business with these technology giants than with traditional incumbent corporations, including financial services providers. Understanding and appreciating this, the tech giants are more and more willing and successfully crossing over into financial services. ApplePay, Amazon Wallet, Google's stunning portfolio of venture capital investments into FinTech, Facebook Chat's endeavors into P2P money transfer, BaiDu (China's dominant search engine) setting up a major online brokerage, Alibaba owning the largest digital wallet in the form of AliPay (well overtaking PayPal) and Tencent running a wide array of financial services through its chat platform WeChat all very clearly indicate that there is growing cross industry convergence from large tech to financial services.

The world's largest money market fund, Yu'E Bao, set up by Alibaba's finance arm Ant Financial in June 2013, now has well over USD 160bn in total assets surpassing JPMorgan's US government money market fund. Yu'E Bao, which means "left-over treasure" is just one of the stunningly rapid growth stories in new finance.

THE GENERATION OF THE SHARING ECONOMY

After experiencing the 2008 credit crisis as young adults, Millennials have gained a strong desire to avoid the mistakes many of their parents made in relation to leverage. For example, when it comes to their cars, instead of leasing like their parents' generation, Millennials tend to turn to alternative solutions such as ride-sharing services like Uber and Lyft in the West and Grab and Didi Chuxing in the East. Instead of taking out a mortgage on a home, statistically Millennials are more inclined to rent an apartment or a house: according to the 'English Housing Survey'. The ratio of households consisting of 25–34-year olds renting their premises increased from 30% in 2005 to 55% in 2015; while owner occupied premises in the same demographic group declined from 70% to 45%. It is also worth to note how this young generation has different spending characteristics: services like Airbnb, clothing swaps, skills sharing, co-working, textbook rental, bike sharing among many others reflect that something has dramatically changed compared to the spending habits of the Baby Boomers. As the 'bon mot' goes: In 1997 the mantra was "don't get into strangers' cars; don't meet people from the internet" in 2017 it is "summon strangers from the internet to get into your car".

The culture of the sharing generation is both directly and indirectly mirrored in financial services such as P2P lending, crowdfunding, P2P investments, P2P money transfer, P2P insurance, P2P leasing, remittances and Application Programming Interfaces opening up banks for communities of developers. It is also notable how Millennials are more open to share data in return for valuable insights: Moven, the famous personal finance dashboard having over two million young users collects and categorizes spending data and provides peer-group comparison for young people about their spending patterns.

THE VISUAL GENERATION

Steve Jobs was one of the few frontrunners intuitively finding out what the future generation demands. As he very well put it 20 years earlier than others realized: "design is not just what it looks like and feels like: design is how it works". This philosophy matches the preferences of the Millennial consumers, having grown up in front of screens (more recently touch screens) where visual information is predominant. Many Millennials have been playing games online with colorful visual, dynamic dashboards and can best understand this genre of communication as opposed to black letters and numbers on a paper printed traditional bank statement. Since their primary screen is the smartphone they appreciate 'portrait' arrangement of visuals over the traditional 'landscape' layout. This is true for text, visuals and even video.

For many Millennials, UX (User Experience) is the new financial services product and they judge UX based on UI (User Interface). UI is basically the design and visualization of information and functions. This is what neo-banks (digital-only banks challenging incumbents by providing only one channel: the smartphone) and PFM (Personal Finance Management) tools focus on. There is a 'bon mot' circulating in Financial Technology circles about what good UI is like: "A User Interface is like a joke. If you have to explain it, it's not that good." Steve Jobs had a rule of thumb which he consistently applied to differentiate 'good' interfaces from 'bad' ones: "when you see it first you have to be able to use it; when you see it second, you have to be able to teach it"—few interfaces by financial services providers can live up to this standard. Simplicity, effortless, and frictionless usage matter, concepts like CES (Customer Effort Score) are on the rise. In wealth management there are efforts to create games that visually drive the user through the price-history of certain stocks. There are also pilot programs which focus on building a virtual 'stock city', where each building represents a publicly traded company, streets are industries, there are districts and the size of the buildings represent total capitalization.

THE SOCIAL MEDIA GENERATION

Facebook had more than 2.4 billion monthly active users as of June 2019—and this one data point tells it all. We are living is a social media world and Millennials are genuinely the native inhabitants of this global virtual universe. This transcends into the financial services industry in multiple ways: ASB Bank opening virtual Facebook branches; ICICI Bank deploying Facebook Pockets providing more than an internet banking integration; users are now willingly and automatically sharing their spending with their social network through Venmo (a highly popular smartphone optimized money transfer arm of PayPal, targeting Millennials). Yet, from a wealth management perspective the non-plus ultra of The Social Media Generation is Social Trading. Social Trading—also known as Copy Trading—is an activity where people use their own profile to trade assets such as stocks, currencies, indices, commodities and ETFs and through a social media interface, can share news, comments, data, ideas, questions, opinions, theories, insights, analysis, pictures and videos among each other. When someone is regarded as a successful investor producing positive returns and providing useful comments, other users can allocate a defined portion of their assets and automatically copy the trades and portfolio of any other user. Successful traders receive asset management fee based on AUM. The undisputed global market leader of social trading is eToro with over six million users globally, yet companies such as Wikifolio, ZuluTrade, Ayondo, Tradeo, Darwinex, SwipeStox, PeepTrade and MyDigiTrade are also notable and each has some unique spin on this new emerging format of online brokerage.

THE DISLOYAL GENERATION

Large corporations from fast moving consumer goods to telecommunications to financial services have quickly discovered that Millennials interacting predominantly through digital channels have significantly higher churn rates than the Baby Boomers. The question is: what to do about it? The answer is the so called 'digital lock-in effect'. The digital lock-in effect creates a situation where the user is inclined to remain loyal to his or her current provider. Best practices are coming from the tech giants. A great example is the Amazon Dash project. Amazon Dash consists of small plastic push-buttons representing particular brand names and equipped with a Wi-Fi connection. These buttons can be placed anywhere in the house of the client. For example, a button with the clients favorite washing powder brand can be placed on the washing machine, another with the preferred beer brand next to the fridge. By pushing the button, the given item automatically pops on the Amazon shopping list of the client. Initial trials in the Silicon Valley were so successful that Amazon Dash Buttons are now available for 300 brands across the USA and UK. The Dash Button creates a strong digital lock-in effect, once the client has the brands of buttons installed across the house, shopping with Amazon becomes so automatic, seamless and personalized that other retailers such as Tesco cannot compete. Digital lock-in effects in the financial services industry can be examined when Millennials use automatic micro-savings products such as Acorns. This service, besides being optimized for smartphone interface, also has a well-designed and useful smartwatch app, where the client can follow purchases and investments. Other similar micro-savings solutions include BankMe, Keep the Change and Way2Save.

Compared to the traditional pre-digital paradigms of customer loyalty which were built on two pillars, emotional and functional benefits, there is now a third pillar emerging: participative benefits. Participative benefits became preeminent in the digital world. Companies running communities of digital brand ambassadors, public chat customer services, interactive Twitter accounts where clients can hashtag the company and report or ask things, user generated content programs and crowdsourcing projects are clearly appreciated by the Millennials. Millennials are 'prosumers' (proactive and interactive consumers) wanting and seeking to be involved in the design and improvement of services they prefer to use. They seek instant two-way channels of public, social, and community communication, something which their parents could never have dreamed of.

SIMPLE WAYS TO CAPITALIZE ON KEY QUALITIES OF MILLENNIALS IN WEALTH MANAGEMENT

	To Do	To Avoid
The Instant Generation	Provide quick and simple fully digital onboarding even if it leads to initially limited functionality.	Processes which can only be done physically or on paper.
The GAFA Generation	Cooperate with large tech companies as well as FinTech startups to provide cobranded or white-labelled services.	Treating business relationships as either 'competitive' or 'cooperative'. The new paradigm is 'coopetition', the active coexistence of competition and cooperation.
The Generation of the Sharing Economy	Set up APIs and proactively motivate third parties to build applications.	Taking unnecessary exposure to P2P lending or crowdfunding—processes often without proper compliance, due diligence and workout. Be careful and selective with involvement in alternative lending as an asset class.
The Visual Generation	Create colorful, visual, well-structured user interfaces. The etalon is the visual world of computer game dashboards—the type of communication Millennials easily and quickly understand. Keep in mind: UX is the new product and UX depends on UI.	Solely alphanumeric representation of data. Reading black and white things is nowadays merely limited to 140 characters. Avoid laptop/desktop focus: in 2016 internet usage via smartphones has overtaken other forms.
The Social Media Generation	Examine the success of social trading sites such as eToro, be excellent in the one social media outlet your potential clients primarily prefer.	Trying to be excellent in all available social media outlets.
The Disloyal Generation	Create ways for your clients to participate in shaping, forming, discussing your product and service.	Avoid trying to mute criticism: Millennials spot this and it is even worse than some critical voices exposed publicly.

PART 4

IT MANAGEMENT, DATA PRIVACY AND REGULATORY IMPLICATIONS

CHAPTER 10

THE REGULATION
OF ROBO-ADVISORS

Richard B. Levin, Peter F. Waltz,
and Robert W. Wenner

Automated financial product advisors, so-called Robo-advisors, are on the advance. Not only have numerous investment advisory firms begun offering such advise through digital platforms, but studies suggest further massive growth. This development poses new questions with regard regulatory frameworks covering this new type of business model. This article discusses the need for regulation and also provides an international perspective.

In recent years, automated financial product advisors, more commonly known as "Robo-advisors" have begun to disrupt the global financial services industry. Using sophisticated algorithms, Robo-advisors are able to advise customers in selecting product offerings including investments, banking products, and insurance policies. Notably, though, the growth of Robo-advisors has posed a challenge to regulators, which have traditionally regulated human intermediaries rather than code.[1]

---

[1] Tom Baker and Benedict Dellaert, *Regulating Robo Advice Across the Financial Services Industry*, 103 Iowa L. Rev. Retrieved from: https://www.law.upenn.edu/live/files/6308-baker-and-dellaert-regulating-robo-advice-across.

WealthTech: Wealth and Asset Management in the FinTech Age, pages 65–71.
Copyright © 2020 by Information Age Publishing
All rights of reproduction in any form reserved.

In early 2017, Michael Piwowar, the acting Chairman of the U.S. Securities and Exchange Commission (the "SEC"), noted:

> As technology continues to improve and make profound changes to the financial services industry, it's important for regulators to assess its impact on U.S. markets and give thoughtful guidance to market participants.[2]

Chairman Piwowar's sentiments were echoed in guidance the SEC later published to the public and registered investment advisers on the growing field of Robo-advisors.[3] This guidance is welcome in an industry that has seen rapid growth over the last couple of years, setting forth a series of recommendations for Robo-advisors to help them meet the disclosure, suitability, and compliance obligations under the Investment Advisers Act of 1940 (the "Advisers Act"). The growth of Robo-advisors has been an international phenomenon, however, and has posed similar challenges for regulators in other countries as they attempt to ensure that their respective regulatory frameworks suit modern technologies.

ROBO-ADVISORS

A growing number of investment advisory firms have begun offering investment advice through digital platforms using proprietary algorithms instead of traditional human advisors. Robo-advisor services are being offered through fully automated means in which the customer only interacts with the digital platform, as well as through hybrid means in which human services are paired in varying degrees with the digital offerings.[4] In both circumstances, the advisory firm is able to offer their services to clients at a lower cost by offering them passive investments that do not need a human adviser and the fees that comes with it. The popularity of Robo-advisors is growing rapidly, with major financial firms such as Charles Schwab and Goldman Sachs developing online advisory platforms.[5] Robo-advisors "create personalized investment portfolios, obviating the need for

---

[2] SEC Acting Chairman Michael Piwowar, SEC Staff Issues Guidance Update and Investor Bulletin on Robo-advisers (Feb. 23, 2017), available at: https://www.sec.gov/news/pressrelease/2017-52.html.

[3] *See Guidance Update: Robo-advisers*, Securities and Exchange Commission (Feb. 23, 2017), available at: https://www.sec.gov/investment/im-guidance-2017-02.pdf and Investor Bulletin: *Robo-advisers*, Securities and Exchange Commission (Feb. 23, 2017), available at: https://www.investor.gov/additional-resources/news-alerts/alerts-bulletins/investor-bulletin-Robo-advisers.

[4] *Can Robo Advisers Replace Human Financial Advisers?* The Wall Street Journal (Feb. 28, 2016), available at: https://www.wsj.com/articles/can-Robo-advisers-replace-human-financial-advisers-1456715553.

[5] *See* Aziz Abdel-Qader, *Goldman Sachs Onboards FinTech Developer as Robo-advisers in The Works*, Finance Magnates (Mar. 21, 2017), available at: http://www.financemagnates.com/fintech/news/goldman-sachs-onboards-fintech-developer-Robo-advisers-works/ and *Hype vs. Reality: The Coming Waves of "Robo" Adoption*, A.T. Kearney 2015 Robo-Advisory Services Study (June 2015).

stockbrokers and financial advisers."[6] A.T. Kearney predicts that approximately USD 2 trn. will be managed by Robo-advisors by 2020.[7]

Proponents of digital investment advice have argued that Robo-advisors are able to handle all of an investor's portfolio needs while keeping costs low and avoiding potentially costly human error and bias that can occur in investment services.[8] Properly constructed and tested Robo-advisors may also help to reduce the incidence of fraud and errors in the provision of advisory services by eliminating humans that are at times driven by greed or other nefarious motives. Critics argue that while Robo-advisors may be able to complement the services provided by traditional human advise, the former will never replace the latter due to the personal element provided by traditional investment services and the nuances involved in investment advice.[9] It is also important to note that, because Robo-advisors are consumer facing products, there are unique risks associated with them. Robo-advisors are well suited to help unsophisticated consumers with investment strategy, given their low costs relative to human advisers. It is critical that as platforms are developed that they take this into account, providing adequate information to inform about a consumer's decision as well as methods to protect consumers who may not always fully understand the nature of the investment activities that they are engaging in.

It is important, however, not to over-react to the growth of Robo-advisors solely because it is relatively nascent technology. Traditionally, investment advisory services have been provided by humans and have been less than perfect. There is reason to believe that algorithms may be able to outperform humans, but the technology likely should not be handed regulatory requirements that go above and beyond those applied to humans, because with all investment there is risk.[10]

Regardless of one's opinion on the virtues of Robo-advise, the recent growth of the industry raises a unique set of regulatory questions and how exactly Robo-advisor services fit under existing supervisory frameworks. Though the SEC has not adopted new rules that are tailored to Robo-advisors, the recent guidance seeks to guide Robo-advisors compliance with existing laws.

EXPLANATION OF BUSINESS MODELS

With the growth of any new product or service offering that falls within the jurisdiction of the SEC and other financial services regulators, it is critical that consumers understand how the services being provided. This is of particular importance with Robo-advisors, as they use technology with which many consum-

---

[6] Nathaniel Popper , *The Robots Are Coming for Wall Street,* New York Times (Feb. 25, 2016), available at: https://www.nytimes.com/2016/02/28/magazine/the-robots-are-coming-for-wall-street.html?_r=0.

[7] Id.

[8] Id.

[9] Id.

[10] See generally supra note 1.

ers may not be familiar. In their guidance, the SEC encourages Robo-advisors to provide clear disclosures, in addition to what is usually required of advisers on the Form ADV, including information about the adviser's specific business model and related risks. Among other items, the SEC noted the disclosures should include "[a] statement that an algorithm is used to manage individual client accounts" and "[a] description of the particular risks inherent in the use of an algorithm to manage client accounts."[11] The SEC believes the disclosures will help to familiarize customers with how Robo-advisors make investment determinations and what specific risks are inherent with such a business model. Robo-advisory products are well-suited for unsophisticated consumers given their costs. Because of this, there is heightened attention that needs to be given to explaining business models and associated risks to consumers.

The SEC believes risks include issues related to algorithms, such as problems with automatic rebalancing of client accounts, or the possibility that an algorithm may not have the capacity to address prolonged changes in market conditions.[12] While Robo-advisors bring added efficiency and cost-effectiveness, the rapid growth of technology and the unique problems inherent in the Robo-advisor business model in the SEC's view justify additional disclosures. It is advisable that when a Robo-advisor is considering the disclosures it plans to make to its customers, to look at the list provided in the SEC's guidance and any unique factors in its product offerings that may create risks beyond what is already noted.

EFFECTIVE COMPLIANCE

Like traditional investment advisers, it is important that Robo-advisors create and maintain thorough internal compliance programs. In the United States, this is set forth by the SEC in Rule 206(4)-7 of the Advisors Act, which requires advisers to establish an internal compliance program to ensure regulatory compliance. Such compliance includes developing policies and procedures "reasonably designed to prevent violations of the Advisers Act" while taking into consideration the nature of the firm's operations and the specific risks that are created. The SEC has noted in specific guidance that the Robo-advisor business model is unique, raising novel compliance concerns. Such concerns include the increased risks created by the Robo-advisor providing advisory services over the internet. The risks should be addressed in the adviser's written policies and procedures and in disclosures to the client regarding changes in the underlying algorithm and the ongoing prevention and detection of cyber security threats.[13] The SEC believes the online provision of advisory services lends itself to compliance that goes beyond the traditional requirements under the Advisers Act. It is critical that Robo-advisors make note of the risks that are inherent in their particular products and services and design a

---

[11] *See supra* note 4.

[12] *Id.*

[13] *Id.*

compliance program that addresses them in sufficient depth and sets forth a plan for continued protections as the underlying technology continues to develop.

TESTING OF ALGORITHMS

An important part of the SEC's guidance on Robo-advisors' compliance programs is the recommendation that Robo-advisors test and back test the code that underpins the algorithms that drive the advisory platform, with continued monitoring of its performance. Digital advisory services offer the potential for great cost-savings and efficiency by using computer programs rather than traditional human advisers. The use of code, however, presents a unique set of challenges to ensure that the advice provided is accurate and that client funds are kept safe. Proper vetting of the code can help mitigate these risks, as can continued monitoring.

The issues that befell Knight Capital Group in August of 2012 provide a clear example of what can happen when algorithms are not properly tested and monitored. Due to an undetected error in the software behind their market-making platform, the group lost $440 million in thirty minutes.[14] The error caused erratic trades to be made on nearly 150 different stocks, buying high and selling low.[15] The error caused a loss that was larger than Knight's market cap of USD 296m. at the time, putting the firm's future in jeopardy.[16] In response in part to the issues that befell Knight Capital Group, the SEC adopted Regulation Systems Compliance and Integrity ("Regulation SCI").[17] Regulation SCI was designed by the SEC to help reduce the occurrence of such issues with algorithms and "improve resiliency when systems problems do occur."[18]

Firms can reduce to the likelihood of such issues through effective testing and monitoring procedures. It is advisable that firms of all size that are entering the Robo-advisor market use caution as they develop the algorithms and software that underlie their services. The SEC notes the importance of testing and monitoring algorithms as a larger component of effective compliance, but likely does not give it attention that it deserves. Given that Robo-advisors target advisory clients, it is critical that the algorithms backing the platforms are sound. Clients need to understand the risks associated with such technology, but it is also imperative that the platforms themselves are doing all that is possible to mitigate risks that stem from their technologies. As the user bases of Robo-advisors grow, so do unique, systemic risks associated with having potentially hundreds of thousands of consumers selecting financial products based on the same or similar models and al-

---

[14] Matthew Philips, *Knight Shows How to Lose $40 Million in 30 Minutes*, Bloomberg (Aug. 2, 2012), available at: https://www.bloomberg.com/news/articles/2012-08-02/knight-shows-how-to-lose-440-million-in-30-minutes.

[15] *See id.*

[16] *See id.*

[17] Regulation SCI: About Regulation Systems Compliance and Integrity, SEC, available at: https://www.sec.gov/spotlight/regulation-sci.shtml.

[18] *Id.*

gorithms.[19] Algorithms are the basis for all Robo-advisor offerings and therefore require critical testing and monitoring to ensure that clients are not improperly advised or that their funds are not misused.

AN INTERNATIONAL PERSPECTIVE

Given the relatively recent rise of Robo-advisors, regulators around the world are working to develop effective systems to oversee their activities. In the European Union (the "EU"), no formal regulatory regime has been put into place, but European supervisory authorities have issued a "Discussion Paper on Automation in Financial Service."[20] The paper seeks comments from consumers and firms to help the agencies identify risks or other areas where specific regulation might be necessary. This is likely a first step in the EU's development of a more tailored regulatory approach.[21]

Australia has taken a different approach. Instead of developing specific regulation for digital advise, the Australian Securities and Investments Commission ("ASIC") has positioned its regulation as "technology neutral."[22] Under this system, the regulations that apply to traditional advisers will also apply to Robo-advisors.[23] A distinction is instead drawn between personal and general investment advice, rather than along technological lines, focusing on competence to provide the advice as well as general compliance measures.[24]

In Hong Kong, no specific action has taken place with regard to Robo-advisors. The Securities and Futures Commission has formed a FinTech Contact Point and Committee, however, with a goal of looking deeper into the regulation of digital investment advice.[25] As the regulations currently stand, though, digital advisory services are regulated under the same regime as traditional investment advice.

The Monetary authority of Singapore (the "MAS"), has developed a regulatory sandbox as an initial step in regulating FinTech.[26] In such a regime, emerging financial products, such as robo-adviers will be able to develop under limited legal and regulatory requirements, in order to both foster growth and allow the MAS to learn more about the industry and how future regulations should be designed.

In the United States, only modest inter-agency regulatory coordination has taken place. Internationally, such coordination is even less developed.[27] Though

---

[19] *See supra* note 1.

[20] *DIGITAL INVESTMENT ADVICE: Robo Advisors Coming of Age*, BlackRock (Sept. 2016), available at: https://www.blackrock.com/corporate/en-at/literature/whitepaper/viewpoint-digital-investment-advice-september-2016.pdf.

[21] *Id.*

[22] Id.

[23] Id.

[24] Id.

[25] See SFC FinTech Contact Point, available at: http://www.sfc.hk/web/EN/sfc-fintech-contact-point/.

[26] MAS FinTech Regulatory Sandbox, Monetary Authority of Singapore, available at: http://www.mas.gov.sg/Singapore-Financial-Centre/Smart-Financial-Centre/FinTech-Regulatory-Sandbox.aspx.

[27] See supra note 1.

there have not necessarily been cases of harm caused by Robo-advisors, regulators should not wait.[28] This technology is growing rapidly and touching more and more consumers, furthering the need for regulation. As with any new technology, the algorithms underlying Robo-advisors are not limited by borders and likely deserve coordinated attention from regulators internationally to both ensure that innovation is fostered and that consumers are protected.

CONCLUSION

The growth of Robo-advisors presents a real opportunity to revolutionize the investment advising business, creating efficiencies and reducing costs. It remains to be seen whether the SEC or other regulators abroad will take specific regulatory action regarding Robo-advisors, but for the foreseeable future they must comply with the Advisers Act and other traditional regulatory frameworks. The SEC's guidance identifies a variety of potential risks the industry must address to comply with the Advisers Act. Successful compliance can be achieved through careful consideration of the risks associated with a Robo-advisor's particular business model and properly crafted disclosure to customers.

Any firm that is planning to offer Robo-advisor services should proceed with caution. Similarly, anyone looking to use Robo-advisor services should make sure the adviser offering the services is registered with.

---

[28] Id.

CHAPTER 11

REGULATING WEALTHTECH AND ROBO-ADVISE IN THE EU

Ulf Klebeck

This work approaches WealthTech and specifically Robo-Advise from a regulatory angle. It discusses the significance of these newly emerging phenomena as well as their target markets and clients. Subsequently it describes the regulatory approach to Robo-Advise as set forth by the EU regulators.

WEALTHTECH AND ROBO-ADVISE: MORE THAN JUST FINTECH BUZZWORDS

WealthTech, defined as the technology sector that focuses on enhancing wealth management as well as its investment process, is more than just a new FinTech buzzword. The same is true for Robo-Advise, which is one of the key ingredients for the rise and success of WealthTech. Admittedly, the most visible players in the WealthTech sector are currently Robo-advisors. There are many different definitions of Robo-Advise[1] but one of the most common defines Robo-Advise as an

---

[1] See ESMA's Final Guidelines on MIFID II Suitability Requirements, 28 May 2018 (hereinafter the "MiFID II Suitability Paper"). https://www.esma.europa.eu/press-news/esma-news/esma-publishes-final-guidelines-mifid-ii-suitability-requirements

WealthTech: Wealth and Asset Management in the FinTech Age, pages 73–82.

online tool that provides automated, algorithm-based advice without or with the limited use of human financial Advisors.[2]

While the US leads the charge in Robo-advise, there is a range of different tools currently available across the globe. Some of the simpler ones are no more than financial calculators allowing the user to see the results of a particular strategy. The more complex tools collect detailed information about an individual's objectives, financial situation, and risk profile and then recommend an asset allocation or strategy that will meet the investor's risk profile and objectives. Some of these tools also recommend particular products to meet the suggested asset allocation, while others facilitate the entire thought-to-investment process by even offering execution services—oftentimes through a third party.[3]

In the recent past there has been a rapid increase in the number of Robo-advise tools available. This seems to suggest that Robo-advise is not just a trend, but a movement that will become an everyday channel for providing financial advice. This has been confirmed by the International Organization of Securities Commissions (IOSCO) in its "Update to the Report on the IOSCO Automated Advice Tools Survey" (published in December 2016).[4] The market for Robo-advise has continued to grow since IOSCO's initial "Report on the IOSCO Social Media and Automation of Advice Tools Surveys" (published in July 2014)[5]—identifying how market intermediaries are using these technologies and how intermediaries and regulators are overseeing their use. What is more, some analysts are anticipating that global spending on digital wealth management initiatives will triple from USD 4bn in 2015 to USD 12bn by 2019.[6]

TARGET MARKETS AND CLIENTS OF ROBO-ADVISORS

According to the IOSCO 2016 survey update, this is mainly due to expanding activity in jurisdictions where Robo-advise was already being provided in 2014, although there has also been an expansion into jurisdictions where Robo-advise was not previously present or allowed. The most obvious target for a Robo-advise tool are "Millennials", the first generation of digital natives. The members of this population segment are most likely to embrace the use of an online tool to manage

[2] See for various definitions of "Robo-Advice" Baker & Dellaert, Regulating Robo Advice Across the Financial Services Industry (2017), Faculty Scholarship, 1740 at 7 et seq., https://scholarship.law.upenn.edu/cgi/viewcontent.cgi?article=2742&context=faculty_scholarship

[3] One could even use the terms "Robo-Advice" and "Robo-Advisor" more broadly to include the similar services emerging in other sectors of the financial services industry, most significantly in insurance, but also in consumer credit; see Baker & Dellaert, Regulating Robo Advice Across the Financial Services Industry (2017), Faculty Scholarship, 1740 at 7 et seq.

[4] See IOSCO's "Update to the Report on the IOSCO Automated Advice Tools Survey Final Report" (FR15/2016; December 2016) at http://www.iosco.org/library/pubdocs/pdf/IOSCOPD552.pdf.

[5] See IOSCO's "Report on the IOSCO Social Media and Automation of Advice Tools Surveys" (FR04/2014; July 2014) at http://www.iosco.org/library/pubdocs/pdf/IOSCOPD445.pdf.

[6] See IOSCO's "Update to the Report on the IOSCO Automated Advice Tools Survey Final Report" (FR15/2016; December 2016) at 19.

their investments. The low cost of Robo-advise as compared to a traditional financial Advisor is also likely to be appealing to this tech-loving generation[7] which is rapidly accumulating assets.

But Robo-advisor tools have far broader potential than just serving the tech savvy generation of Millennials. Institutional investors, such as pension funds and endowments, are also looking to Robo-advise tools to give their members and clients more control over their investments. This does not mean that Robo-advisors will completely replace human advisors. Instead, it is likely that there will always be a market segment that prefers interaction with real people. Clients requesting human interaction may be of slightly older, slightly wealthier demographic, or they simply enjoy strong, trusting relationships with their financial advisors. Finally, the appeal of a robo-advise tool may lie in the fact that it can also be used in combination with a human financial advisor. This is the model that Vanguard has successfully adopted in the US. When used in conjunction with an advisor, a Robo-advisor also serves as a useful compliance mechanism—keeping a detailed record of a customer's objectives, financial situation, and risk profile and providing a check on what the Advisor has recommended.[8]

THE WEALTHTECH CHALLENGE FROM AN EU REGULATORY PERSPECTIVE

Having Robo-advisors supporting human advisors follows the old principle: "If you can't beat them, join them!". But join in what? This leads to the first and most fundamental challenge of the current FinTech and thus WealthTech discussion— i.e. the question of properly delimiting the business scope of WealthTech as well as Robo-advise. And one has to admit: There is no clear and precise definition or categorization. Whatever (sub-)categories of FinTechs one defines, e.g. WealthTech, InsureTech, RegTech, Blockchain, Distributed Ledger Technology, the lines will be increasingly blurred over time. Business models that evolved pre-digitalization defined the historical financial services categories—i.e. retail, private and investment banking, wealth and/or asset management—and with that (more or less) the applicable financial market regulation in the EU. But FinTechs do not stop at old boundaries among categories. Rapid improvements in technology are enabling financial services' business models that were not possible 15 to 20 years ago. These innovations in finance operate within a regulatory system which is coming from the analogue world and is struggling to keep pace with the new developments coming from the digital world.[9] ESMA (the European Securities and Markets Authority), one of the 3 pan-European Supervisory Authorities

---

[7] See Klebeck & Dobrauz, FinTechs im Lichte und Schatten des Aufsichtsrechts—quo vadis EU?, RdF 2015, at 276 et seq.

[8] See Jackson-Maynes, The rise of Robo-Adice tools in financial planning (July 2015) at http://www.kwm.com/en/au/knowledge/insights/rise-Robo-advisor-tools-financial-planning-20150716.

[9] See Klebeck & Dobrauz, FinTechs im Lichte und Schatten des Aufsichtsrechts—quo vadis EU?, RdF 2015, at 277 et seq

(so called "European Supervisory Authorities), was spot-on when it confessed that the existing EU regulations were not necessarily designed with the digital industry in mind.[10]

WealthTech, like any other sub-set of FinTech, represents a challenge to regulators in many ways—and vice versa. Both sides are asking, which regulatory authorities govern and supervise FinTechs? Which rules do FinTechs have to abide by? Which FinTech has to adhere to which regulation? Small service providers struggle to navigate a complex, ever-increasing regulatory environment as they attempt to define their own compliance model. The same is true for long-standing players struggling to keep up with the increase of financial market regulations in the EU. Ultimately, regulators are facing the challenge of creating an uneven playing field between the traditional service providers, i.e. human financial advisors, and the WealthTech solution providers—by applying (or not) financial market regulations to the traditional and/or new players.[11]

Even if regulators and supervisors seem to have a natural tendency to search for risks and concerns with regards to financial innovations, the pan-EU regulators declared a different objective. They aim to tackle the subject of FinTech applying a balanced approach, both "protective and supportive".[12] The challenge is not only to identify when the regulator should step in, but also how to take regulatory action.[13] In general, regulators can take one of three approaches: (1) ban or restrict products, business models or processes, in the light of the potential risks (restrictive approach); (2) take a "wait and see" approach (watchful approach) and/or (3) actively facilitate and regulate the product, business models or process because of its potential economic and social benefits (facilitative or catalyst approach) and/or because of known threats to the regulator's objectives.[14]

---

[10] See See manuscript of the speech of Verena Ross (Executive Director at European Securities and Markets Authority) at London Business School/ Bank of England Conference on Date (07 March 2016; ESMA/2016/345): "How Imminent is the real FinTech Revolution, Financial Innovation: towards a balanced regulatory response" (https://www.esma.europa.eu/sites/default/files/library/2016-345_financial_innovation_towards_a_balanced_regulatory_response_-_speech_by_v._ross_0.pdf), at 9.

[11] See Klebeck & Dobrauz, FinTechs im Lichte und Schatten des Aufsichtsrechts—quo vadis EU?, RdF 2015, at 278 et seq.

[12] See manuscript of the speech of Verena Ross (Executive Director at European Securities and Markets Authority) at London Business School/ Bank of England Conference on Date (07 March 2016; ESMA/2016/345): "How Imminent is the real FinTech Revolution, Financial Innovation: towards a balanced regulatory response" (https://www.esma.europa.eu/sites/default/files/library/2016-345_financial_innovation_towards_a_balanced_regulatory_response_-_speech_by_v._ross_0.pdf).

[13] See also Arner, Barberis & Buckley, FinTech, RegTech and the Reconceptualization of Financial Regulation, at 38 et seq.

[14] See e.g. for ESMA's approach the manuscript of the speech of Patrick Armstrong, Senior Risk Analysis Officer, Innovation and Products Team at ESMA, at Oslo Børs ASA: Stock exchange and Securities Conference: "Financial Technology: Applications within the Securities Sector" (23 January 2017; ESMA71-844457584-330): https://www.esma.europa.eu/sites/default/files/library/esma71-844457584-330_speech_fintech_and_asset_management_by_patrick_armstrong.pdf, at 3.

At EU-level the European Supervisory Authorities have taken, for now, mainly the second approach towards financial innovation. There is a need to better understand the various innovations and their possible applications in the financial market. The pan-EU regulators actively attempt to learn more about an innovation at hand. However, they do so only as long as this innovation remains sufficiently immature to ensure that they are not placing their key objectives of stability, protection, and integrity at risk by not taking action. By waiting to see how the innovation develops the EU regulators strive not to risk stifling a potentially socially or economically useful product, business model or process. Apparently at EU level the innovations coming from FinTech have not reached the "tipping point" where active regulatory participation is required.

LATEST REGULATORY DEVELOPMENTS FOR WEALTHTECH—AN OVERVIEW

In December 2015, the Joint Committee of the three European Supervisory Authorities launched a discussion paper on the topic of automation in financial advice, which offers an illustrative example of the European regulatory approach towards Robo-advise. The Discussion Paper explained the concept of automated advice and highlighted the potential benefits and risks to consumers and to financial institutions. The aim of this paper was to assess what, if any, regulatory or supervisory action is required to mitigate potential risks and at the same time how best to harness the potential benefits of this innovation.[15]

Among the benefits repeatedly highlighted, was that this newly discovered method of delivering financial advice can potentially provide inclusion to consumers previously excluded from professional financial advice. Additionally, this expanded access to financial advice comes at lower costs and with the potential to deliver highly consistent consumer experiences for those seeking financial advice. Other possible benefits relate to the standardization that automation can bring, which can result in a more consistent consumer experience. A fully automated and standardized advisory process can also facilitate record-keeping, allowing institutions to more easily check and audit the quality of the advice they have provided.

The results of the discussion paper[16] highlight certain risks inherent to the automation of financial advice compared to traditional "human" professional advice: first, the risk that consumers could misunderstand advice provided to them with-

---

[15] On December 2016, the Joint Committee of the European Supervisory Authorities published a Report on automation in financials advice: https://esas-joint-committee.europa.eu/Pages/News/European-Supervisory-Authorities-publish-conclusions-onautomation-in-financial-advice.aspx. The Report followed the public consultation on the "Joint Committee Discussion Paper on automation in financial advice" published by the three ESAs on December 2015, available on: https://www.esma.europa.eu/document/discussion-paper-automation-in-financial-advice.

[16] See the Report of the Joint Committee of the European Supervisory Authorities published on automation in financials advice: https://esas-joint-committee.europa.eu/Pages/News/European-Supervisory-Authorities-publish-conclusions-onautomation-in-financial-advice.aspx

out the benefit of a professional advisor to supporting them throughout the advisory process; second, the potential for limitations or errors in automated tools; and third risks associated with the widespread use of automated advice tools, for example the possibility of a "herding risk" if a significant volume of consumers end up transacting in the same way in relation to the same financial products and services. But as of now, no immediate action has been taken at the EU level.

Given that there is no specific regulatory framework for Robo-advise tools in Europe, Robo Advisors must fit themselves within the existing regulatory regime for financial advisors in Europe. Yet, EU legislation with regards to Robo-advise differs depending on the product and distribution model. However, the principal financial services legislation relevant for advice on securities products is the Markets in Financial Instruments Directive ("MiFID II") and for insurance-based products is the Insurance Distribution Directive ("IDD"). Although these regulatory frameworks for investment services with regards to securities and insurance products generally apply, there are still some gaps or inconsistencies when investment advice is provided on an automated basis.

Broadly speaking, Robo-Advisory services for securities products will require a license in an EU member state pursuant to the local implementation of MiFID II from 1 January 2018, if they constitute the provision of "personal recommendations in relation to transactions in financial instruments" or meet conditions for certain ancillary services. Robo-advise relating to the insurance would be subject to registration requirements, information requirements and conduct of business obligations under the IDD, if they constitute "insurance distribution" but no authorization requirement exists unless the distributor is an insurance company to which Solvency II applies.

Other legislation may be relevant in relation to specific products or clients, e.g. the Undertakings for Collective Investment in Transferable Securities (UCITS) IV Directive and the Alternative Investment Funds Manager Directive (AIFMD) for funds or the Regulation for Packaged Retail and Insurance-based Investment Products (PRIIP) from 1 January 2018, and consumer protection measures where services are provided to individuals.

With regards to these existing regulations and regulatory developments in the EU there are a number of practical considerations that providers of Robo-Advisory services need to consider. For example, how will more technology-reliant models of Robo-advise satisfy the need to ensure suitability and appropriateness of the investment products being offered? How is ensured that advice is in accordance with the requirements under MiFID II? How should liability be attributed where the service relies on third-party-algorithms or technology which falls short of the required standards? Once a Robo-advise tool qualifies as investment advice or portfolio management under MiFID II, the firm providing the advice has to comply with the provisions of MiFID II, in particular with the requirements of the suitability assessment—as highlighted by ESMA in its MiFID II Suitability Paper.[17]

ESMA[18] argues that the use of automated tools for the provision of invest-ment advice and portfolio management services might raise some specific issues related to the protection of investors. In particular, it seems possible to identify at least three main areas where specific needs of protection may occur: (1) The information that should be given to clients on the investment advice and portfolio management services when these services are provided through an automated tool (this concerns both, which information should be provided as well as how infor-mation should be illustrated to clients); (2) The assessment of the suitability (with particular attention to the use of online questionnaires with limited or without human interaction); (3) The organizational arrangements that firms should imple-ment when providing Robo-advise.

On the first aspect, ESMA highlights in its MiFID II Suitability Paper[19] that firms rendering Robo-advise should be aware that the ability of a client to make an informed decision might be based solely on electronic disclosures. These disclosures are potentially made via email, Websites, mobile applications and/or other electronic media. Unlike the traditional (face-to-face) investment advice and portfolio management services, the Robo-advise may not provide initial or subsequent conversation with a person when collecting information about the cli-ent. The degree of human interaction available to investors may substantially vary from one platform to another. Some outlets may offer the opportunity to contact the advisory firm's staff (also this aspect may vary; employees may be available by email, phone or for limited in-person meetings); others may only provide tech-nical support. In some cases, the human interaction offered to clients may vary depending on the account size or the invested amount.[20]

When assembling the information to be provided to clients, firms should there-fore consider how to explain their automated model and the purpose of the in-vestment advice. This information as well as the portfolio services themselves should be yielded in a clear and simple manner so that it easily comprehensible for potential clients. The information given to potential clients should also in-clude an explanation of the degree of human interaction available to clients. This is particularly important in order to clarify the means through which clients can gain access to an investment firm's personnel, should this option still be available. Moreover, firms providing Robo-advise may or may not make staff available to clients to highlight and explain important concepts and to reply to questions when clients are responding to an online questionnaire. Conversely, clients may not read or fail to understand disclosures that are not phrased in plain language and therefore potentially not user-friendly. Firms should therefore consider how to

---

[17] See MiFID II Suitability Paper.
[18] See MiFID II Suitability Paper.
[19] See MiFID II Suitability Paper.
[20] See MiFID II Suitability Paper.

present all relevant information to clients and put the necessary arrangements in place to provide clients online with fair, clear and non-misleading information.[21]

Secondly, ESMA observes that the advice provided to investors through automated tools might be elaborated primarily, if not solely, based on the clients' previous responses to online questionnaires. However, online questionnaires may vary with respect to length and the types of information requested. Some questionnaires may provide the client with the opportunity to provide additional information/explanation or context regarding the feedback that the client gives. As services provided may be entirely automated, preventing the investment firm's personnel to ask follow-up or clarifying questions about the client's responses contingency planning is of high importance. Firms should address inconsistencies in client responses, or provide the client with help when filling out the questionnaire.[22]

Lastly, ESMA believes that firms providing Robo-advise should design and implement organizational arrangements taking into account the peculiarities of their business model. For example, the reliance on algorithms, the limited human interaction with clients (if any), and the provision of investment advice over the internet may create or accentuate risk exposure for the firm that should be addressed through written policies and procedures. ESMA has expanded on some of the existing guidelines and has included examples to provide some practical guidance, on how to apply the MiFID II requirements on suitability, to firms providing investment advice or portfolio management through automated or semi-automated systems.[23]

Furthermore, ESMA emphasizes that firms should pay particular attention on how information on the suitability assessment and its purpose is provided. This is all the more important in such circumstances where only very limited interaction with the firm's personnel (or none at all) may take place. Given the specific features of Robo-advise and the related investor protection issues that may arise when using such tools, guidance and practical examples have been added. These are meant to ensure that firms provide clients with comprehensive information to allow them to understand the purpose of such tools. For example, it is particularly important that clients are informed on whether the investment firms foresee human interaction in the investment process or not. If so, the firm should also disclose the degree of human interaction it envisages and how the client can get in touch with the relevant personnel.[24]

Finally, ESMA notes that further examples of the information that firms may provide to clients potentially include an explanation of the purpose of the algorithm used to provide the investment advice or the portfolio management services (e.g., that the algorithm generates recommended investments; that individual cli-

---

[21] See MiFID II Suitability Paper.
[22] See MiFID II Suitability Paper.
[23] See MiFID II Suitability Paper.
[24] See MiFID II Suitability Paper.

ent accounts might be invested and rebalanced by the algorithm); a description of any circumstances that may cause the firm to override those algorithms (e.g., that the algorithm might freeze trading or take other temporary defensive measures in stressed market conditions); a description of any involvement by a third party in the development, management, or ownership of the algorithm. This may also include an explanation of any conflicts of interest such an arrangement may create.[25]

In this regard it should also be noted that the details provided in the mentioned guidelines solely focus on the features of Robo-advise, given its innovative nature and its growing relevance as a means to provide investment advice and portfolio management services. Nevertheless, ESMA stresses that those guidelines are not intended to be exhaustive. Further obligations to disclose information on the services rendered may exist, pursuant to Article 24 of MiFID II and the related provisions of the MiFID II Delegated Regulation.

SUMMARY AND OUTLOOK

At EU level there is currently no coherent regulatory concept in the area of digital financial services—including WealthTech and Robo-advise. Specific FinTech regulations approaches exist only in certain areas.[26]. But there is more to come! The strategy paper of the European Commission on a single digital market for Europe promotes the creation of a "digital single market" in response to the increasing digitization of the EU economy and of society. Naturally, this will also affect FinTech. This fact has also recently been acknowledged by the European Parliament, one of the EU law-making institutions. To the EU Parliament FinTech constitutes a building block of modern digital society. The EU needs this building block in order to withstand the competition from the rest of the world.[27] Therefore it has been recommended that the European Commission, another EU law-making institution, should present a comprehensive action plan that boosts FinTech in Europe—whether separately, or as an integral part of two recent initiatives at EU level to deepen EU's single market idea. FinTech shall be included into the further strategies of the Capital Markets Union[28] and Digital Single Market[29] strategies. This commitment to FinTech has been confirmed by the recently published consultation document of the European Commission "FinTech: a more competitive

---

[25] See MiFID II Suitability Paper.
[26] See Klebeck & Dobrauz, FinTechs im Lichte und Schatten des Aufsichtsrechts—quo vadis EU?, RdF 2015, at 278 et seq.
[27] See European Parliament (Committee on Economic and Monetary Affairs), Draft Report on FinTech: the influence of technology on the future of the financial sector (27 January 2017;2016/2243(INI); http://www.europarl.europa.eu/sides/getDoc.do?type=COMPARL&reference=PE-597.523&format=PDF&language=EN&secondRef=01), at 3.
[28] For an overview, initiatives and development of the EU Capital Market Union strategy see http://ec.europa.eu/finance/capital-markets-union/index_en.htm.
[29] For an overview, initiatives and development of the EU Digital Single Market strategy see https://ec.europa.eu/commission/priorities/digital-single-market_en.

and innovative European financial sector"[30] as well as by the commissioning of an internal task force on FinTech.[31]

To date, these initiatives remain only legislative "declarations of intent". Currently the EU is still holding back on any regulatory activism. A coherent Fin-Tech-dedicated regulatory concept is not yet on the EU's horizon. However, once a WealthTech service provider, in particular a Robo-advise tool, qualifies as providing investment advice or portfolio management under MiFID II, the firm has to comply with the provisions of MiFID II. Along with that the service provider will face a series of new regulatory obligations it has to comply with. Among those will be client segmentation/classification, codes of conduct as well as best execution obligations, the duty to provide certain information to clients and last, but not least, the requirements of the suitability assessment under MiFID II. Going forward, the regulatory debate on WealthTech and Robo-advise in the EU will need to be conducted in light of MiFID II.

---

[30] See European Commission's public consultation on FinTech: a more competitive and innovative European financial sector: https://ec.europa.eu/info/finance-consultations-2017-fintech_en.

[31] See European Commission's announcement on its website: https://ec.europa.eu/digital-single-market/en/blog/european-commission-sets-internal-task-force-financial-technology.

CHAPTER 12

PROTECTION OF PRIVACY FROM CONCEPTION OR PRIVACY BY DESIGN

Nicolas Steiner

"Privacy by design" is a widely misused term. What does it cover and how can it be ensured that vendors comply with the principles suggested by it? Breach response procedures as well as privacy impact assessments are two key components of the General Data Protection Regulation. In addition, Blockchain technology can help to address some data privacy related issues for financial services firms, such as cross border financial transactions.

PRIVACY BY DESIGN?

"Protection of privacy from conception" is not only a widely misleading term, but how to ensure that suppliers truly comply with the principles set forth by this term is a difficult undertaking and it requires a nexus of actions.

For a long time, we were witnessing a 'patch culture'. That is an attitude that companies have known for many years and which forces them to spend more time maintaining their information systems than launching new projects. The practice has become so commonplace that CIOs wait several months or even years after the launch of a new solution to start operating it, until the relevant supplier has

WealthTech: Wealth and Asset Management in the FinTech Age, pages 83–86.
Copyright © 2020 by Information Age Publishing

made the necessary adjustments to deploy the new offering. The cloud, however, is about to bring changes to this situation.

The Software-as-a-Service (SaaS) mode has indeed changed the status quo. If software vendors continue to evolve their solutions over time, these changes are made in a completely transparent fashion and are provided in such a way that users no longer have to go through lengthy and laborious testing and deployment phases, Instead, they can take advantage of a system update immediately. This mechanism is now fully supported by the supplier, however, a fundamental problem remains:

The functional improvements typically meet new user expectations, while at the same time the security features attempt to tackle issues that have not been as clearly pinpointed and communicated until then. This presents a vulnerability which pirates may have exploited in the meantime. This issue becomes particularly critical when the solution deals with personal data.

THE PRIVACY FUNDAMENTALS

To solve this problem and to guarantee the protection of the user privacy, it is necessary to get to the root causes of any potential privacy violation. It is from that very observation that the concept of "privacy by design" was born. Here, the idea is to integrate privacy measures into the design of any solution.

One principle is therefore to not require the user to take action if he or she disagrees to personal data being collected, stored, and exploited by a software provider. The personal data collected shall only encompass those pieces of information absolutely necessary for the requested service.

Before moving further, it is helpful to take a closer look at the fundamentals underpinning user identity management. Kim Cameron, who led the Microsoft Architecture with Bill Gates, addressed the missing identity layer of the Internet with a defined number of laws intended to overcome various digital identity and privacy issues.

In reference to the Kim Cameron's seven "Laws of Identity" any vendor is required to natively follow seven fundamental principles of safety when designing a product on a conceptual level:

1. Proactive not reactive; preventative not remedial
2. Privacy as the default setting
3. Privacy embedded into design
4. Full functionality—positive-sum, not zero-sum
5. End-to-end security—full lifecycle protection
6. Visibility and transparency—keep it open
7. Respect for user privacy—keep it user-centric

It remains to be seen whether a vendor from which a company intends to source services will truly comply with these rules. To verify this a key document should be consulted: binding corporate rules (BCR), developed by the European Union.

The BCR can be seen as "a code of conduct, defining the policy of a company in terms of transfers of personal data".[1] For an actor based in the United States and offering a cloud-based content management platform, offering its users complete and transparent BCRs is an essential element of trust. And this is all the more the case as, according to customer requests, storage can be located in the United States, or strictly outside.

The BCRs are structured around 12 rules that establish basic principles on compliance with local regulations, transparency on the use of personal data, respect for individual freedoms as well as operational commitments.

"Privacy by design" is not limited to technical questions of encryption or authentication which are now largely mastered, but it requires a specific organizational setups and processes. This is why we currently observe an increasing level of Chief Privacy Officer (CPO) being appointed coupled with a team of key legal and compliance experts.

Their sole task is to ensure that the policies for protection of personal data are properly applied. They ensure a constant monitoring on the data usage, implement the evolutions in the regulations and answer the questions of the customers, employees, and partners on these subjects.

The team is also responsible for raising the awareness of all employees on the issue of privacy. Each employee follows a training program on international legislation, Internet policy, and audit rules. Moreover, they are being introduced to rules of engagement with supervisory institutions. In this way, privacy is no longer one solution among many others, but the entire organization that embodies "privacy by design".

A relatively new technology that can help to meet the requirements of General Data Protection Regulation (GDPR) and support to strike the right balance between "legitimate privacy" and GDPR in the wealth management industry is the Blockchain or Distributed Ledger technology (DLT). Some people hold that innovations such as Bitcoin which operates on a public Blockchain network was any money-launderer's "weapon of choice". Yet, it is the very attributes of this technology that—when applied to wealth management and core banking—will help data controllers to satisfy new requirements set forth by the regulator. In particular the function of pseudonymization, the science of using cryptography to legitimately obfuscate identity, will help to meet the GDPR requirements. Much work is being done to bring the benefits of this technology to the mainstream, most notably by the R3CEV consortium and the open source Hyperledger project. There is a lot of activity ongoing in Switzerland in this sector and is home to organizations such as Ethereum which has created a language set for smart contacts.

---

[1] https://inform.tmforum.org/features-and-analysis/2017/05/getting-ready-gdpr-privacy-design/

The country is also home of many proof of concepts (PoCs) and projects under way in the WealthTech area aiming to deliver solutions to the wealth management industry. Moreover, the Swiss watch and micro electronic industry dedicates significant resources to address digital identity use case with connected objects. A case in point is the recent joint announcement of Swisscom and the Centre for Digital Revolution (C4DR) that they would closely collaborate. Over the next few years we will witness the rise of these new technologies helping organizations to meet the regulatory requirements while at the same time offering a better range of products and services to discerning wealth management clients.

Looking forward, "privacy by design" should be fully integrated across different digital platforms with an Open API layer. New technology companies such as Consekense are making their platform available to corporate clients willing to outsource innovation and test the digital value chain by producing PoCs outside their own company infrastructure. This facilitates the aggregation of the drivers forming a connected innovation ecosystem and will be used to test new collaborative patterns brought on by the digital distribution models.

REFERENCES

Binding Corporate Rules
    http://ec.europa.eu/justice/data-protection/international-transfers/binding-corporate-rules/index_en.htm
Laws of Identity by Kim Cameron
    https://msdn.microsoft.com/en-us/library/ms996456.aspx
R3CEV consortium
    https://www.r3.com
Hyperledger
    https://www.hyperledger.org
Ethereum project
    https://www.ethereum.org
Entrepreneurship Institute @Level39
    http://entrepreneurshipinstitute.co.uk
Consekense
    http://www.consekense.com
Centre for Digital Revolution
    C4DR.com
Collaboration announcement between C4DR and Swisscom
    http://www.cityam.com/265267/eric-van-der-kleij-ex-level39-and-tech-city-boss-back-new)

PART 5

FINANCIAL RISK AND PERFORMANCE MEASUREMENT

CHAPTER 13

HOW CAN ROBO-ADVISORS HELP TO ENHANCE INVESTMENT RETURNS?

Claus Huber

It is often difficult for investors to assess which Robo-advisor's asset allocation approach delivers the most favorable long-term performance. This paper addresses this need by comparing different asset allocation and rebalancing methodologies that are utilized by Robo-advisors and their impact on risk/return and drawdowns with empirical data.

The introduction of a new technology is generally accompanied by skepticism and low acceptance. Given that the first Robo-advisors only came to market in 2008, they still have to achieve mainstream status with retail investors as well as institutionals. One concern that so regularly raised pertains to the difficulty for investors to assess which asset allocation approach applied by Robo-advisors delivers the most favorable long-term performance. This paper addresses this need by comparing different asset allocation and rebalancing methodologies that are utilized by Robo-advisors and their impact on risk/return and drawdowns with empirical data.

The first methodology is a 60% equities and 40% bonds allocation (henceforth referred to as 60/40) that rebalances quarterly. For the example of a Swiss inves-

WealthTech: Wealth and Asset Management in the FinTech Age, pages 89–93.
Copyright © 2020 by Information Age Publishing

89

tor, the portfolio would comprise an Exchange Traded Fund (ETF) on the SMI with a weight of 60% and an ETF on Swiss government bonds with a weight of 40%. Investors rebalance quarterly to bring their exposure back to the original 60/40 allocation. If, for example, equity markets rose during the last quarter more strongly than bonds, parts of the equity ETF would be sold, and the proceeds spent to increase the holdings of the bond ETF.

The second methodology investigated here adjusts exposure according to market volatility on a quarterly basis, i.e., it reduces exposure to equities and bonds when volatility rises. It is therefore called the Target Volatility strategy. Robo-advisors typically ask investors to fill in a questionnaire to determine their risk appetite. After answering a series of questions, including the client's investment horizon in years, some Robo-advisors assign the investor a target volatility. For instance, the longer the investment horizon, the higher the target volatility. Suppose that the investor´s target volatility was set to 8% based on the questionnaire. This along with a mid-level risk tolerance is resulting in the same 60% equities and 40% bonds allocation as the 60/40 strategy. If the portfolio´s volatility increases to 16% at the end of one quarter, however, Target Volatility would reduce exposure to equities and bonds to 30% and 20%, respectively. The remaining 50% capital would be invested in cash. By contrast, irrespective of the level of market volatility, the allocation of the 60/40 strategy without Target Volatility remains at 60% equities and 40% bonds. Generally, the sum of all weights cannot exceed 100%.

The 3rd methodology utilizes the Buy&Hold strategy as passive benchmark, where the investor at the beginning of the investment period buys for 60% of his assets an ETF reflecting the investor's domestic equity market and for 40% an ETF representing the domestic bond market. No rebalancing takes place during the investment period. More asset allocation models are investigated in the extensive study by Huber (2017).

DATA

The data sample (Table 13.1) contains monthly returns for the 5 countries Germany, USA, United Kingdom, Japan and Switzerland. The equity indices of these countries are represented by the MSCI net return equity indices Standard (Large+Mid Cap) in local currency. They include dividend payments after taxes and were available from 12/1969 to 10/2016. For the government bond markets of these countries, total return indices from Citigroup's Yieldbook comprising bonds with maturities between 7 and 10 years in local currency were taken. These indices were available from 1/1985 to 10/2016. In order to gauge the long-term performance of the discussed strategies when implemented with ETFs, management fees of 0.30% for equities and 0.20% for bonds as well as transaction costs of 0.15% for both equities and bonds were deducted.

TABLE 13.1.   Descriptive Statistics for Equity and Bond Indices of the 5 Countries, 1/1987—10/2016

	Germany		US		UK		Japan		Switzerland	
	Equities	Bonds	Equities	Bonds	Equities	Bonds	Equities	Bonds	Equities	Bonds
Total Return	6.2%	6.5%	9.3%	6.9%	8.5%	8.2%	0.7%	4.4%	7.2%	4.7%
Excess Return	2.6%	3.0%	5.9%	3.5%	2.6%	2.4%	−0.4%	3.3%	4.8%	2.3%
Volatility	21.2%	4.8%	15.1%	6.3%	15.3%	6.1%	19.7%	5.0%	16.3%	4.0%
Sharpe Ratio	0.12	0.62	0.39	0.56	0.17	0.39	−0.02	0.67	0.29	0.57

RESULTS

Our Target Volatility approach calculates at the end of each quarter the realized volatility based on monthly data with the exponentially weighted moving average (EWMA) method and decay parameter $\lambda = 0.8$. With $\lambda = 0.8$, effectively no more than 24 historical observations are included in the volatility estimation. Admittedly, this a very simplistic approach to forecast volatility, and more sophisticated models could have been applied. However, the goal of this study is to gauge the performance of intuitive and simple to implement rebalancing strategies. Given that 24 monthly returns were needed to estimate the first volatility for 1/1987, 358 monthly returns from 1/1987 to 10/2016 comprise the database. Quarterly rebalancing means that 120 portfolio adjustments were conducted and for each rebalancing date volatilities and correlations were estimated.

The target volatilities for each country were set to 75% of the country's domestic 60/40 strategy. In Figure 13.1, the respective target volatility is given after the country's name: for example, as the German domestic 60/40 investor's realized volatility is 12.5%, his target volatility was set to 0.75 * 12.5% ≈ 9%, which translates into [DE 9%]. The target volatility for the Japanese investor was also set to 9%, for the Swiss investors to 8% and those for the UK and the US to 7%. Figure 13.1 exhibits drawdowns on the X-axis and the Sharpe Ratios on the Y-axis for each of the 5 countries. The average of the 5 countries is displayed in the upper left panel. The metric "Drawdown" symbolizes the average of the 5 largest drawdowns suffered by the strategies during the period 1/1987 to 10/2016. A drawdown measures the loss suffered by an investment from a valuation peak to a valuation trough and can last several months of even years. The Sharpe Ratio measures risk-adjusted returns and is defined as SR $= (r_p - r_f)/\sigma_p$, where r_p is the return of the portfolio, r_f the return of the risk-free asset, and σ_p the portfolio's volatility. The higher the Sharpe Ratio and the lower the drawdowns, i.e., the closer to the right corner the results are in Figure 13.1, the more favorable is the result.

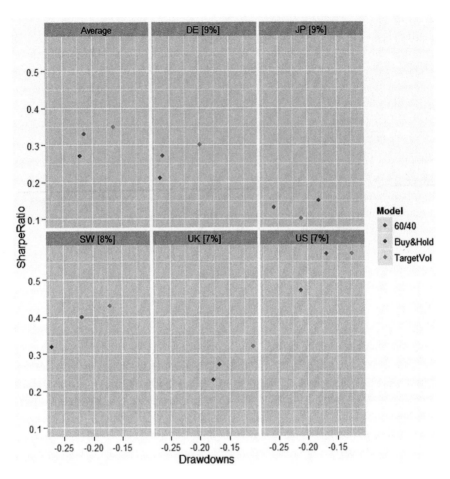

FIGURE 13.1.   Drawdowns vs. Sharpe Ratios for the 5 Countries and Different Rebalancing Models

For all countries but Japan the Target Volatility approach (blue dots) achieves the best results, followed by 60/40. Again, with the exception of Japan, Buy&Hold comes in last. Target Volatility's performance advantage is economically signifi-cant: for example, for the average of the 5 countries, the average of 5 worst draw-downs is reduced from –22% for Buy&Hold to –16% for Target Volatility. 60/40 (–21%) is only marginally better than Buy&Hold. Applying the 60/40 and Target Volatility strategies enhances Buy&Hold's Sharpe Ratios by 0.08 to 0.10. Given that the average Sharpe Ratio for the 5 countries is 0.27, this is a significant im-provement.

Buy&Hold invests in 1/1987 and leaves the portfolio unchanged until 10/2016. Buy& Hold will perform most strongly in secular bull markets. One example could be equities rising in a long-term trend and simultaneously outperforming bonds. Then the weight of equities would increase from 60% to a higher portion over time. In contrast, the regular rebalancing of 60/40 leads to selling equities in a rising market and buying them in a falling market and hence will perform best in markets with more pronounced up and down swings. Target Volatility strategies will perform well relative to 60/40 and Buy&Hold if equity markets fall and volatility becomes elevated, which is usually the case during times of market stress. By analogy the Target Volatility strategy increases asset weights if markets normalize and volatility recedes.

This article addresses the need of investors to gauge the usefulness of different asset allocation and rebalancing methodologies as applied by Robo-advisors. Simulations based on historical data from 1987 to 2016 show that the suggested Target Volatility strategy outperforms the 60/40 strategy as well as the Buy&Hold method. It achieves not only higher Sharpe Ratios but also lower drawdowns. The conclusion and recommendation for investors is hence to look for Robo-advisors that adjust asset allocations dependent on market volatility, for example, with a Target Volatility approach.

REFERENCE

Huber, C. (2017). *Target volatility: Are there benefits for domestic and international investors?* https://papers.ssrn.com/sol3/papers.cfm?abstract_id=2977841

CHAPTER 14

PERFORMANCE WATCHER

Nicholas Hochstadter

Switzerland is a major global hub for wealth management. As such its wealth management industry is heavily impacted by technological developments in that sector.
Against this backdrop performance management in the wealth and asset management industry is also undergoing major changes. More importantly the methods for
measuring performance must also be adjusted for the new WealthTech age.

Wealth management in Switzerland is a gigantic market. The numbers are almost
dizzying. Between banks and asset managers, nearly CHF 7,000bn are deposited
and administered in the country. This amount corresponds to half of the US GDP
or, for local comparison, to more than ten times the Swiss GDP.

Switzerland controls one quarter of the global wealth management market.
This leadership role has been maintained, even with the negative impact of
the financial crisis. The wealth under management fell by approximately CHF
5,000bn immediately following the financial crisis, but during the past five years
has steadily been returning to its record levels of 2007. On the other hand, in the
"engine room", technology has been lagging behind.

In the age of FinTech and its ultra-light applications, Swiss wealth management is still entangled in legacy systems that some have compared to the archaic
apparatus of the London underground. The problem lies not in the lack of tools,
since they already exist, but rather in the difficulties encountered in adopting them
and exploiting them to the best of their potential.

The most obvious delay is in the information that Swiss managers deliver to their customers. Information and technologies—these are two concepts with which Swiss financial organizations maintain a rather distant relation to. In the management reports sent to customers, unfortunately, the data provided tends to the minimal. If performance is a fundamental criterion of motivation and satisfaction for customers, it is surprising that it is so inadequately reported.

This situation cannot continue, given the profound changes that have affected other sectors. With the advent of big data and social networks, where everything is instantaneous on the Web, information of any kind cannot remain isolated or withheld.

To fully understand the limitations of wealth management in reporting, it is enough to compare its applications to that of its big sister, asset management (investment funds). Under the supervision of the regulator, the asset management sector demonstrates much more transparency and forward development, until. Month after month, fund managers detail their results extensively. Sharpe ratio, Treynor ratio, max drawdown, annualized performance over 1 year, 3 years, 5, sectoral and geographical allocations: performance is dissected from every angle. Further, managers also indicate how they rank within their peer group. They measure themselves against each other without hesitation. Total transparency is required. As a result, investors have all the information needed to make informed decisions about the products that best match their profile and goals.

This cannot be said for the area of private wealth management where performance is not prominently displayed. Private investors do not necessarily need the mass of information provided to institutional investors, but they are still entitled to a minimum service that has yet to be standardized.

In most cases, reporting is limited to gross returns, in the absence of any value scale. Risk measurement, if only through volatility, or performance contributors, only rarely appears on radar screens. Benchmarking relative to the risk managers take to produce returns or performance for similar investment styles is lacking. Comparisons are out of the question. On its own, performance or performance information is only of relative value. It only makes sense when it is placed in a certain context.

Initiatives such as Performance Watcher have been designed for this purpose. These new community-based solutions are based on information sharing and allow the online performance of securities portfolios to be measured and compared online. It has the advantage of integrating the risk parameter into the equation, and of measuring the quality of the return only after taking into account the volatility associated with it. By working this way, sudden performance spikes are immediately highlighted, which may seem positive at first glance, but which may actually be due to excessive risk taking. These sites, where an increasingly large community of individuals and professionals are growing together, allow each other, in an anonymous manner, to compare the performances obtained in identical management styles, according to risk tolerance thresholds.

Until a few years ago, expensive software was needed to harvest, process and distribute this sensitive data. Today, ultra-light applications—and also ultra-secure—exist to accurately manage all these flows. There is, therefore, no reason for wealth management to escape methods that have already had a profound impact on other sectors. The digital revolution has opened a new era, that of hyper-information. What follows is an era of hyper-consumption, which the sociologist Jean Baudrillard called the code of "personalization". "No individual in itself is dependent on it," he went on, "but he goes through every individual in his relationship to others."

Forty years after Baudrillard, this formula can also be extended to the Web and social networks. It is those players who generate this hyperinformation. Every minute, the Facebook community is exchanging several million documents in multiple forms. Between LinkedIn, Twitter, Facebook and others, there are billions of documents on the Web to publish, edit, share, reformat and redistribute, information which marketers are keen to gather and interpret.

Previously, in the marketing world, information flows circulated in one direction, from producer to consumer. Today, the patterns are reversed to the point that consumers have become their own media. The buy-side emits just as much content as the sell-side. For areas such as travel, appliances, electronics, furniture, and entertainment among many others, it is no longer possible to buy anything without the buyers mingling their voices with those of the sellers. Both have become inseparable.

Approximately three years ago, an advertising campaign of CSS Assurances proclaimed that modernity requires that hospitals can be chosen based on recommendations by their patients. Ten years ago, this concept was unthinkable. Today, comparison sites, from Booking.com to Kelkoo, have become obligatory points of passage. There is no reason to believe that wealth management can escape these modes of recommendation. Here, modernity could very well consist in selecting a bank or a manager based on its client's recommendations. The wealth management industry will not be able to escape this development.

It must be understood that investment performance, and the reporting of this performance, has only a relative value. More than merely having access to this information, customers want to have confidence in those who deliver the information to them. In general, and this is the very principle of the media, information is not only of practical value. It is also and ultimately of great relational value, as it allows the creation of the link. The purpose of initiatives such as Performance Watcher is not just to communicate the risk-adjusted returns generated by the portfolio managers. The purpose goes beyond this. It is to create, or recreate, relationships of trust between managers and customers. During the last decade, following the financial crisis, this trust has at times disappeared. Customers have become extremely suspicious and risk management has become a business in its own right.

Trust, as much as performance, is at the heart of the relationship that is established between the manager and his client. For Gurviez and Chorka, two academics, trust is based on the notions of reliability, credibility, integrity, and a certain amount of benevolence, that the customer perceives in the person who offers him his products or services. This is exactly what the FinTechs can and should do. Thus, the real innovation and added value of applications such as Performance Watcher, is to give the investment managers a platform where they can demonstrate they consider the interests of their customers and to deliver on the investment promises that have been made. FinTech becomes a voice that allows its users to hold a constructive conversation and to build the trust upon which managers base their value proposition. By appearing on these platforms, managers do not guarantee that they will be the performance leader, but they reinforce their commitment to satisfy their customers.

There is still some way to go before Performance Watcher conquers its market in the manner of a Tripadvisor or a Twenga, however, the financial industry, without being fully aware of it, is already going down that path. Today, these applications gather diverse and varied profile information without it being possible to draw up a precise typology. Tomorrow, the new modes of communication and information flows will be such that they will lead to a specialization of practices. In the family of wealth managers, the cards will be redistributed. Managers will focus on the area where they generate the highest added value, which is not always the case today. In the near future, performance and trust segmentation will most probably decide the division of roles.

Some managers will focus on managing financial assets and others on the customer relationship and quality of service. The former generates trust the latter creates confidence as they will be able to rely on the work of the former, and vice versa. Managers, whether they reside in banks or in management companies, will certainly not disappear, but it soon time for them to reorganize their ranks.

PART 6

THE COMPETITIVE LANDSCAPE

CHAPTER 15

CROSS BORDER SET UP OF CROWDLENDING INVESTMENT FUNDS

Torsten Ries

Crowdlending platforms experienced strong growth in the recent years. Lenders and borrowers, however, are facing dedicated challenges given the fact that a uniform legislation does not exist, if at all. The author is therefore proposing an intermediation between lenders, platforms and borrowers by implementing an investment fund structure in compliance with European investment and fund regulation.

NATURE AND REGULATORY FOUNDATION OF INVESTMENT FUNDS

Nature, design and set up of undertakings for collective investments ("UCIs" or "funds") are predominantly determined by the content and conditions of their respective fund regimes or laws, legal forms and fund types [1]. Investment guidelines and –restrictions which determine the fund's strategy (investment policy) can generally be freely defined by the fund's initiator (and therefore form the fund's character and distinguishing features). Dedicated investment restrictions may, however, arise from specific national and cross-border directives, regulations and laws or may be given by allocation bandwidths or diversification requirements respectively.

WealthTech: Wealth and Asset Management in the FinTech Age, pages 101–108.
Copyright © 2020 by Information Age Publishing
All rights of reproduction in any form reserved.

"Investment law regulates the activities of asset managers when managing the funds of [...] pooled (collective) investments of multiple investors." [2]. The dominant fund types within the European Union are "Untertakings for Collective Investments in Transferable Securities" (UCITS) [3] as well as "Alternative Investment Funds" (AIFs) [4] [5].

The relation between involved parties within a fund set up is characterized by contractual relations between intermediaries (e.g. the fund's depositary bank) and investors as well as between intermediaries among each other (e.g. between the fund's management company and the fund's depositary bank) [6]. These contractual relations between involved counterparties may be visualized by an isosceles investment triangle which includes the fund's legally required service providers as well as optional external and delegated counterparties such as portfolio managers, investment advisors, prime brokers, administrators, distributors, etc. (Figure 15.1).

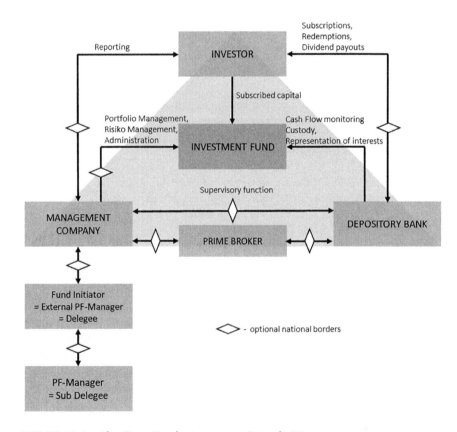

FIGURE 15.1.   The Cross-Border Investment Triangle [8].

Over the years very few countries have emerged within the European Union as dedicated fund administration centers (especially Luxembourg which holds a market share of 26.5 % of the European Investment Fund Industry [7]) resulting in the fact that contractual and economic relations between a fund's counterparties are predominantly characterized by cross-border relationships; the strong trend of specialization and focusing on specific functions as well as European fund and investment law's objectives underpin this development.

FINTECH AND THE CLASSIFICATION OF CROWDLENDING PLATFORMS

Delineation of Terms and Segmentation

There is no uniform definition of "FinTech", especially as the development of financial services and technical applications is ongoing. Simplified "FinTech", a contraction of "Financial technology", refers to technology enabled financial solutions." [9]. More precisely *Dhar* and *Stein* define FinTech as "financial sector innovations involving technology-enabled business models that can facilitate dis-intermediation, revolutionize how existing firms create and deliver products and services, address privacy, regulatory and law-enforcement challenges, provide new gateways for entrepreneurship, and seed opportunities for inclusive growth." [10].

Corresponding to this definition, Internet businesses took a tremendous development over the recent years resulting in Internet-based platforms (such as Amazon, PayPal, eBay, Expedia, Facebook, etc.) which have become commonplace in almost all areas of commerce [11]. An Internet platform as such may be defined as "[…] an entity that "facilitates exchange between two or more independent groups usually consumers and producers, using a combination of channel access, functionality embedded in an IT system, and associated key business processes (sometimes augmented with physical assets)." [12].

The FinTech industry can be divided into four major segments: "financing", "asset management", "payment instructions" as well as "other FinTechs" [13]. *Dorfleitner, Hornuf, Schmitt* and *Weber* classify "Crowdlending" as a sub segment of "Crowdfunding" which as such may be described as "[…] a form of financing in which a large number of contributors […] provide the financial resources to achieve a common goal." [14].

The Concept of Crowdlending

The general concept of Crowdfunding is following the idea of collective intelligence. "Crowdfunding promises to democratize financing processes and create a level playing field for competing ideas." [15]. Crowdlending (also referred to as "FinTech Credit", "Peer to Peer Lending" or simplified "P2P" [16]) as a part of the Crowdfunding concept takes up this idea and is driven by the goal to enable credit (or loan) activity between borrowers and lenders over electronic platforms bringing together the borrower's credit demand and the lender's appetite to invest in credit facilities. Both, lenders and borrowers, need to register on the credit platform which matches their supply and demand of credit respectively. Lenders may be individual persons as well as legal persons, namely institutional investors, corporates, investment funds, etc. On P2P platforms various credit segments are supported "[…] including consumer and business lending, lending against real estate, and non-loan debt funding such as invoice financing." [17].

Investors may acquire (i) whole loans or (ii) fractions of loans. While option (i) leads to a "one-to-one" relationship between the lender and the borrower, option (ii) results in a "one-to-many" relationship as various lenders contribute to the loan sum requested by the borrower. In doing so it is not guaranteed that the borrower is finally receiving the requested credit amount. The borrower eventually needs to accept the credit amount the crowd is willing to provide. Many platforms encourage their investors to invest in several credits in order to diversify their risks [18]. As part of the platforms' onboarding process borrowers will be classified based on numerous criteria and information they need to provide to the platform. As a result of the platforms' analysis and assessment of the received information the borrower receives a platform specific credit rating which is decisive for the borrower's risk scoring and finally the amount of the interest rate he has to pay to the lenders. Depending on their risk appetite lenders may decide to invest in loans with dedicated risk-reward profiles expressed through the dedicated credit rating tranche in which the specific loan is ranged in. Some platforms offer automated allocation features to auto-select loans with specific risk-reward ratios in order to build-up a specific loan portfolio.

Granted loans are mainly based on loan agreements. These agreements include the loan conditions as well as the repayment provisions. Interest payments as well as repayments are typically paid to the lender whereas the platforms receive servicing fees and commissions as part of the interest payments and repayments or as a credit discount (or premium) to be carried by the borrower.

Beside economic (business) and liability reasons, the various models employed depend on national regulatory requirements which may vary strongly from country to country. Five main variations of Crowdlending platforms may be differentiated [19].

1. The *traditional P2P lending model* provides for a direct relationship between the borrower and the lender whereas the platform delivers credit risk analysis to the lender and investment information to the borrower. The loan is finally originated by the investor (lender, creditor).
2. The *notary model* foresees a matching service for lenders and borrowers and corresponds mainly to traditional P2P lending model. On the contrary the platform is partnering with a fronting bank which is finally originating the loan to the borrower.

3. The *guaranteed return model* corresponds to the traditional P2P lending model whereas the platforms guarantees interest payments and repayments. As in the traditional model the loan is finally originated by the lender.

4. According to the *balance sheet model* the platform itself is originating the loan from its balance sheet. Claims (e.g. interest payments and repayments) may then be assigned to investors whereas cash flows are routed over the platform.

5. Enterprises using the *invoice trading (or factoring) model* may sell dedicated invoices to platforms with a discount. Investors may then acquire the invoices (or receivables) offering the selling enterprise immediate liquidity.

Despite the advantages and growth of the P2P lending industry in the recent years the Crowdlending industry is facing dedicated challenges [20]:

- From an investor perspective agency costs include the potential lack of information on the credit rating model applied by the respective platform. In addition to that young platforms lack a lending history which makes it difficult for them to assess historical default rates of borrowers.
- The assumption of adverse selection problems may lead to high interest rates and low success rates.
- In order to assess the Crowdlending market's development and information provided by platforms lenders need to observe the market and evaluate respective analyses. As the transparent supply of information is leading to extensive information for lenders it may get difficult for investors to take efficient decisions.
- The Crowdlending market is national and therefore does not provide for uniform and consistent rules and prerequisites. In addition to that P2P platforms use different models for assessing the borrower's credit rating which makes it difficult for investors to compare credit offerings from different platforms.
- Given the aforementioned aspects investors may face difficulties to create an efficient and risk adjusted diversified credit portfolio.
- The Crowdlending industry is largely unregulated which may make it difficult for lenders to enforce their rights.
- The risk of borrowers which may be unable to finance their projects to completion may lead to illiquid and / or defaulting loans.

CROWDLENDING INVESTMENT FUNDS

By implementing Crowdlending investment strategies, investment funds may constitute a regulated and institutionalized vehicle to face some of the aforementioned challenges. Given the European investment and fund laws' anatomy, a fund

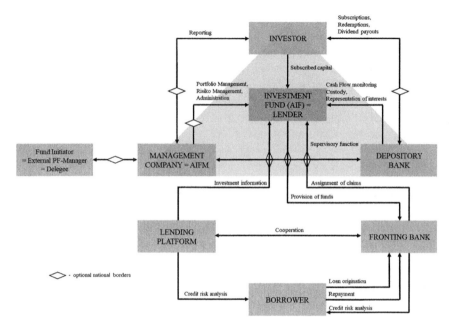

FIGURE 15.2.

setup as an AIF may be taken into consideration. In contrast to a direct investment investors may choose to invest in a regulated AIF which in turn takes on the position as the lender. The AIF may consequently act as lender on various platforms in different countries. Lending platforms as well as involved intermediaries and counterparties (e.g. the delegated portfolio manager or the fund's management company) may be located in different countries; therefore cross-border aspects like the applicability of International Private Law as well as national laws need to be considered with regard to the legal and tax structure of the AIF.

ENDNOTES

[1]   AV Akademikerverlag, Saarbrücken. Figure following Zetzsche, D. (2015). IPR im Investmentdreieck von Anlegern, Fondsverwaltern und Verwahrstellen.

[2]   Zetzsche, D. (2017). *The anatomy of European investment fund law* (April 12, 2017). Available at SSRN: https://ssrn.com/abstract=2951681.

[3]   Directive 2009/65/EC of the European Parliament and of the council of 13 July 2009 on the coordination of laws, regulations and administrative provisions relating to undertakings for collective investment in transferable securities (UCITS). Retrieved from: https://eur-lex.europa.eu/legal-content/EN/ALL/?uri=CELEX%3A32009L0065

[4]   Directive 2011/61/EU of the European Parliament and of the Council of 8 June 2011 on Alternative Investment Fund Managers and amending Directives 2003/41/EC and 2009/65/EC and Regulations (EC) No 1060/2009 and (EU) No 1095/2010. Retrieved from: https://eur-lex.europa.eu/legal-content/EN/TXT/?uri=CELEX%3A32011L0061

[5]   For a comprehensive overview of European fund law see Moloney, N. (2014). *EU Securities and Financial Markets Regulation* (3rd ed.). United Kingdom: Oxford University Press.

[6]   For a detailed evaluation of the anatomy of collective investment vehicles see Zetzsche, D. (2015). *Prinzipien der kollektiven Vermögenanlage*. Tübingen: Verlag Mohr Siebeck.

[7]   European Fund and Asset Management Association. (September 2017). Quarterly statistical release (No. 70, p. 14). Retrieved from: http://www.efama.org/Publications/Statistics/Quarterly/Quarterly%20Statistical%20Reports/170918_Quarterly%20Statistical%20Release%20Q2%202017.pdf.

[8]   Figure taken from Ries, T. (2017). *Delegationen im Privatrecht der Kollektivanlangen* (p. 50). AV Akademikerverlag, Saarbrücken. Figure following Zetzsche, D. (2015). *IPR im Investmentdreieck von Anlegern, Fondsverwaltern und Verwahrstellen*.

[9]   Arner, D. W., Barberis, J. N., & Buckley, R. P. (2015). *The evolution of FinTech: A new post-crisis paradigm?* University of Hong Kong Faculty of Law Research Paper No. 2015/047; UNSW Law Research Paper No. 2016-62, p. 1. Retrieved from: SSRN: https://ssrn.com/abstract=2676553.

[10]   Dhar, V., & Stein, R. M. (2016). *FinTech platforms and strategy*. MIT Sloan Research Paper No. 5183-16, p. 2. Retrieved from: SSRN: https://ssrn.com/abstract=2892098.

[11]   Dhar, V., & Stein, R. M. (2016). *FinTech platforms and strategy*. MIT Sloan Research Paper No. 5183-16, p. 3. Retrieved from: SSRN: https://ssrn.com/abstract=2892098.

[12]   Dhar, V., & Stein, R. M. (2016). *FinTech platforms and strategy*. MIT Sloan Research Paper No. 5183-16, p. 4. Retrieved from: SSRN: https://ssrn.com/abstract=2892098.

[13]   Dorfleitner, G., Hornuf, L., Schmitt, M., & Weber, M. (2016). *The FinTech market in Germany* (p. 5). Retrieved from: SSRN: https://ssrn.com/abstract=2885931

[14]   Dorfleitner, G., Hornuf, L., Schmitt, M., & Weber, M. (2016). *The FinTech market in Germany* (p. 5). Retrieved from: SSRN: https://ssrn.com/abstract=2885931

[15]   Zetzsche, D.A., & Preiner, C.(2017). *Cross-border crowdfunding—Towards a single crowdfunding market for Europe* (p. 6). European Banking Institute Working Paper Series 2017—No. 8; University of

Luxembourg Law Working Paper No. 2017/002; European Business Organization Law Review, Forthcoming; Center for Business & Corporate Law (CBC) Working Paper 003/2017. Retrieved from: SSRN: https://ssrn.com/abstract=2991610.

[16] Committee on the Global Financial System (CGFS) and the Financial Stability Board (FSB). (2017). *FinTech credit.* Retrieved from: http://www.fsb.org/2017/05/fintech-credit-market-structure-business-models-and-financial-stability-implications/

[17] Committee on the Global Financial System (CGFS) and the Financial Stability Board (FSB). (2017). *FinTech credit* (p. 1). Retrieved from: http://www.fsb.org/2017/05/fintech-credit-market-structure-business-models-and-financial-stability-implications/

[18] Committee on the Global Financial System (CGFS) and the Financial Stability Board (FSB). (2017). *FinTech credit* (p. 12). Retrieved from: http://www.fsb.org/2017/05/fintech-credit-market-structure-business-models-and-financial-stability-implications/

[19] For a detailed description of the following models please refer to Committee on the Global Financial System (CGFS) and the Financial Stability Board (FSB). (2017). *FinTech credit* (p. 11–17). Retrieved from: http://www.fsb.org/2017/05/fintech-credit-market-structure-business-models-and-financial-stability-implications/

[20] Please see Fenwick, M., McCahery, J. A., & Vermeulen, E. P. M. (2017). *FinTech and the financing of entrepreneurs: From crowdfunding to marketplace lending* (pp. 25, 26). TILEC Discussion Paper No. 2017-25; ECGI—Law Working Paper No. 369/2017; Lex Research Topics in Corporate Law & Economics Working Paper No. 2017-3. Retrieved from: SSRN: https://ssrn.com/abstract=2967891.

[21] Following the notary model showed in graph 3: stylized notary model in Committee on the Global Financial System (CGFS) and the Financial Stability Board (FSB). (2017). *FinTech credit* (p. 13–17). Retrieved from: http://www.fsb.org/2017/05/fintech-credit-market-structure-business-models-and-financial-stability-implications/

[22] Acc. to Art. 21 para. (5) lit. (a) AIFM-D, Art. 23 para. (1) UCITS-D the depositary is the only counterparty within a fund's service provider set up which must have its domicile in the same country as the fund itself.

[23] Compare Art. 4 para. (1) lit. (w) in connection with lit. (a) und (b) AIFM-D). Conditional is Art. 20 para. (2) lit. (b) AIFM-D.

CHAPTER 16

THE LANDSCAPE OF ROBO-ADVISOR OPERATORS IN THE DACH REGION

Maryna Tykholoz-Cukov

This text provides an overview of the main market players in the asset and wealth management industry providing Robo-advisory services in the DACH region (Germany, Austria and Switzerland). The author characterizes and compares conditions offered by Robo-advisor operators of all versions (Robo 1.0, Robo 2.0, Robo 3.0 and Robo 4.0). Upon writing this text there are 13 operators in Germany, 13 in Switzerland and 5 in Austria.

The value of assets under management (AuM) of European Robo-advisors is quite modest in comparison with global figures. The general number of Robo-advisor operators in the European wealth management market is comparatively small and is comprised of approximately 73 organizations at the present time.

The center of Robo-advisor in Europe is traditionally located in Great Britain, with the vast majority of providers based in London. However, the DACH region is expanding quickly in this area. There are currently more than 32 Robo-advisors registered in the DACH region and many more in start-up mode.

In terms of AuM, it is fair to note that the company Feelcapital EAFI SL. from Spain (with EUR 1 bn) is the largest market player as of today. Nutmeg from the

WealthTech: Wealth and Asset Management in the FinTech Age, pages 109–114.

UK is also a major player with approximately EUR 650 mn in AuM. There are four further companies which have crossed the EUR 100 mn AuM milestone: Scalable Capital GMBH (Germany), CheBanca (Mediobanca Group, Italy) and Moneyfarm (Italy and Great Britain) and Pritle (Netherlands). More companies are expected to cross this milestone; however, as the industry continues to grow, the European market dispersion will change.

The following paragraphs aim to analyze the offerings of the largest Robo-advisor operators in DACH region.

GERMANY

The very first Robo-corporate startup in Germany was Quirion, a by-product of Quirin Bank. Later Commerzbank established the subsidiary FinTego. Deutsche Bank developed a cooperation with the FinCite as a white label solution to offer

TABLE 16.1.   The Summary Data of the Biggest Robo-Advisors in Germany as of August 1, 2017

Name	Founded	Located	Minimum Account, Offering
1822direkt	2014	Frankfurt a.M.	No minimum account; Banking services; General investment accounts
Scalable Capital	2014	Munich	Minimum account EUR 10 000; General investment accounts
A.IX Capital	2014	Dusseldorf	Minimum account EUR 50; General investment accounts; Advisory services
Cashboard	2014	Berlin	Minimum account EUR 1; General investment accounts; Guaranteed +2% on the first EUR 10 000; EUR 50 welcome bonus
Dein Anlageberater.de	2016	Traunstein	Advisory services; Five available packages
Easyfolio	2009	Frankfurt a.M. München Stuttgart	Minimum account EUR 100; General investment accounts at one of partner banks
Ginmon	2015	Frankfurt a.M.	Minimum account EUR 5000 or EUR 1000 with a reinvestment of EUR 50 per month; General investment accounts
Growney	2014	Berlin	Minimum account EUR1; General investment accounts; EUR 50 welcome bonus
LIQID	2015	Berlin	Minimum account EUR100000; General investment accounts
Vaamo	2013	Frankfurt a.M.	No minimum account; General investment accounts
Visualvest	2015	Frankfurt a.M.	No minimum account; General investment accounts
Whitebox	2014	Weil am Rhein	Minimum account EUR 5000; No fees for the first 6 months; General investment accounts
Quirion	2013	Berlin	Minimum account EUR10000; General investment accounts; Personal advice per phone EUR150/h

their maxblue AnlageFinder. Almost at the same time the number of Rob-startups like Cashboard, Growney, Scalable Capital, Whitebox and others entered German market in 2014.

German Robo-advisors managed approximately EUR 1m of AuM at their dawn in 2013, EUR 30m in 2014 and grew to EUR 170m in 2015 (M. Dorfleitner, G., Hornuf, 2017, p. 36). The list of Robo-advisors in Table 16.1 provides mainly advisory services (DeinAnlageberater.de) or offer accounts in German banks. Their specialty is that many of them require no or a small minimum account size due to the competitive market and high price sensitivity of customers. German market fees range from 0, 10% to 0, 99% of investable assets. DeinAnlageberater.de is the cheapest operator providing paid individual investment advice for up to fifty different options. The leader in terms of AuM is Scalable Capital GmbH which provides the Robo 3.0, has many affiliated companies, and has approximately 50 employees.

Ginmon can be categorized as Robo 3.0. This company offers both portfolio proposals and capabilities for creating and managing investment accounts. It partners with online brokers such as DAB bank and bank Consors.

Vaamo (Robo 3.0) is another well-known service based on a high level of peoples' trust. The company only earns fees when clients increase their accounts; so, it eliminates all possible conflicts of interest.

SWITZERLAND

The Swiss wealth management market has always been densely stuffed with long-standing traditional advisors including private banks and investment companies. Many of these institutions are known world-wide and have won the trust of their customers for decades. Yet, following the introduction of negative interest rates for savings accounts on 18 December 2014, the search for other investment opportunities was reinforced. The Swiss banking market remains the most challenging market due to its legal banking secrecy.

The general market tendency indicates that Robo-advisor operators in Switzerland are registering at a lagging rate compared with other European countries. Further, startups are experiencing competition from the Swiss banks which have introduced their own e-services. Therefore, the majority of the Robo-advisor service providers currently belongs either to affiliated companies of large established financial institutions (TrueWealth, SimpleWealth) or the proprietary e-solutions of large established financial institutions (UBS Advice, CS Invest Solutions, Investomat).

The company InvestGlass was the first platform providing tailor made automated advice on asset re-allocation and docile products in the version Robo 2.0. This company does not target investors which seek fully automated portfolio rebalancing but rather those investors looking for automated tailor-made suggestions on how to improve their portfolio management. The Robo-operators charge mostly fixed fees for their services on a monthly or yearly basis. According to the estimation of the largest providers, the Swiss Robo-advisor market needs approximately CHF 1bn of assets under management (AuM) in order to be profitable.

Beside fees and minimum account size, most Swiss Robo-companies require investors to have a permanent Swiss residence due to the financial regulations of the Swiss banks where their accounts are held. Table 16.2 highlights the Swiss Robo-advisor operators that are either active or in the process of launching.

VermögensZentrum VZ Group, founded in 1993, is a large Swiss financial services company listed on Swiss Exchange (SIX). The company mainly specializes in the areas of portfolio management and retirement planning for wealthy individuals (age 50 or older) as well as in pension fund management and insurance for companies with more than 20 employees. It has started online advisory services for its clients which pay consulting and management fees. This company has branches in 26 cities in Switzerland.

TABLE 16.2. The Summary Data of the Robo-Advisors in Switzerland as of August 1, 2017

Name	Founded	Located	Minimum Account, Offering
Vermögens Zentrum "VZ Financial portal"	2010	Zurich	No minimum account; Investing in local companies; General investment accounts
Glarner Kantonalbank "Investomat"	2015	Glarus	Minimum account CHF 5000; Services only for residents; General investment accounts
True Wealth	2013	Zurich	Minimum account CHF 8500; General investment accounts; Passive indexed products
Swissquote	1999	Zurich	No minimum account; Online banking and brokerage services; Services only for residents
InvestGlass	2014	Geneva	Minimum account CHF 200000; General investment accounts; 14 days free trial
DeinAnlageberater.ch GmbH	2015	Altendorf	Advisory services; Five available packages
Simple Wealth	2015	Zurich	Minimum account CHF 5000; Services only for residents; General investment accounts
Descartes Finance	2015	Zug	Minimum account CHF 5000; Diversified investment accounts
UBS Bank; "UBS Advice"	2015	Zurich	Minimum account CHF 1500 and CHF 1m for non-residents; Diversified investment accounts
PostFinance Bank	2017	Bern	Launch process starts in 2017
Julius Bär; "Your Wealth"	2017	Zurich	Launch process until 2018
Werthstein	2016	Zurich Germany	Launch process started
Leodan Hybride Privatbank	2015– 2016	Zurich	Closed because of legal sentencing; Automated and human advice

The Glarner Kantonalbank, operating since 1884, has gained recognition with its online financial services that were introduced to the market. It provides not only online asset management "Investomat" but also online mortgages "Hypo-mat", online savings accounts "Kontomat" and online life insurance "Risikomat".

One of example of a young Robo-advisor is Werthstein, founded by former private bankers from Germany and Switzerland. The technology platform was developed by the large Swiss FinTech company "Additiv". Additiv has been consulting and assisting banks in technological solutions since 1998.

It is worth mentioning that in the area of fees, Robo-advisor providers are also disrupting the Swiss traditional wealth managers by often charging their clients lower prices for comparable services.

AUSTRIA

The Austrian market of Robo-advisor is rather uncultivated at the moment. The main players are mostly big international companies that provide services in Vienna as well as in other big European cities. The fees for their services vary. Consequently, Table 16.3 highlights the few active operators in the Austrian market the majority having another country of company origin.

Novofina is a startup company established by an Austrian trading. It is the most Austrian authored company in the Table. Novofina claims to be the next 4.0 generation of Robo-advisor. The Company does not hire customer support agents but retains only professional staff. It provides self-developed algorithm-based solutions that can scan the portfolio of every client and open and close positions without human communication. Novofina's self-developed algorithms have been. confirmed by more than 10000 simulated back-tests of live trading results.

TABLE 16.3. The Summary Data of the Biggest Robo-Advisors in Austria as of August 1, 2017

Name	Founded	Located	Minimum account, offering
Novofina	2014	Vienna; Berlin; Zurich	Minimum account EUR30000; General investment accounts
Scalable Capital	2014	Vienna; Munich	Minimum account EUR10000; General investment accounts
ETFmatic	2014	16 EU cities	Minimum account EUR1000; General investment accounts, ISA, Junior ISA
Ginmon	2015	Frankfurt a.M.	Minimum account EUR 5000 or EUR 1000 with a reinvestment of EUR 50 per month; General investment accounts
Growney	2014	Berlin	Minimum account EUR1; General investment accounts; EUR 50 welcome bonus

Forward-looking Robo-advisors are increasingly collecting comprehensive financial data from their clients through the aggregation of account, investment and payment information in a digital and easily accessible way. The added value for their clients will be the ability to receive better analysis of their saving and investment behavior, cash flow forecasts, and real time proposals for and saving and investment options.

REFERENCE

Dorfleitner, M., Hornuf, G., Schmitt, L., & Weber, M. (2017). *FinTech in Germany.* Cham, Switzerland: Springer International Publishing.

CHAPTER 17

DOOMED LIKE DINOSAURS

Patrick Schueffel

The dinosaurs found a rather abrupt ending as they were not able to adjust to changing environmental conditions. In this section it is argued that wealth and asset managers may face similar consequences if they show no ability to adjust. In particular
the effects of client unhappiness, demographic and societal shifts, and changes of
technology are elaborated.

Around 65 million years ago the extinction of the dinosaurs started. 200 years later the dinosaurs were gone. It is still uncertain what precisely triggered the short-
taken die-off of the dinosaurs. What is undisputed, however, is that the rather
sudden change of environmental conditions caused the extinction of this species.
The dinosaurs simply did not have enough time to adjust to the new environment
by evolution.

Several trends that fuel the development of FinTech have the potential to alter
the business environment for asset managers as sudden and as dramatically as it
happened to the dinosaurs. Those trends are client unhappiness, demographic and
societal shifts, and technology.

CLIENT UNHAPPINESS

In 2008 clients across the globe suffered from a blow to their financial assets.
Many clients started asking themselves why they are paying professionals hefty

fees for managing their assets and yet were still caught on the wrong foot. But the ramifications of the global financial crisis went far beyond a monetary drawdown. People started asking more fundamental questions about the role of financial intermediaries in general. This led to business models sporting the democratization of investment such as crowd financing and crowd investing. Moreover, the repercussions of the crisis were longer lasting than expected. Today's zero interest environment still causes asset managers and clients alike to pull a long face.

DEMOGRAPHIC SHIFT AND SOCIETAL SHIFTS

It is no secret that many societies in western countries are ageing at an unprecedented speed. Ever fever working individuals are tasked with supporting an ever-larger crowd of retirees. But the ratio of working to non-working population is just one aspect. The other factor amplifying the problems caused by increasing longevity are snowballing healthcare costs that need to be shouldered somehow. Yet, whilst we see aging societies in the western world, we see growing middle classes in eastern societies, such as China. A larger affluent segment is now the basis for a bigger demand for asset management services.

TECHNOLOGY

Today's standard smart phone has a memory that is about one million times larger than the computer that put the Apollo mission on the moon. At the same time, it is approximately 800 times faster but costs only a tiny fraction of the Appollo Guidance Computer. This impressive technological progress renders possible not on only entirely new distribution channels on the front end, but also novel business processes on the backend. Artificial intelligence will increasingly influence portfolio management, virtual agents with speech recognition capabilities will gradually take over customer support and advanced analytics will become the standard to crunch big data whilst using the resources of the cloud. APIs will ensure a seamless integration of IT even across company borders.

INTERPLAY OF TRENDS

Some of these trends will also reinforce each other. For instance, unhappy clients are not expected to become much happier any time soon in view of a zero-interest environment that makes it virtually impossible for them to generate interests for their retirement.

Furthermore, the dramatic demographic shift will also cause a large share of assets to be passed on to a younger generation soon. The younger generation is not only more tech-savvy than the older ones, but they will also demand an entirely new type of user experience, most likely device-based and self-directed. The generation that grew up with Google, Facebook, and iPhone is less likely to keenly interact face-to-face with a grey-haired representative of the financial services industry.

FinTech firms strive in these conditions. Building on latest technology they help unhappy clients to tap into new sources of interest, they promise to be more transparent and to charge lower fees than incumbents. New financial planning tools provided by FinTech firms as well as performance comparison portals sooth the worries of troubled pension savers. Robo-advisors are providing affluent clients with wealth management services which were previously confined to high-net worth individuals. By doing so they increasingly poach in the preserve of traditional asset managers.

NOW OR NEVER

Incumbent wealth and managers now have the chance to embrace these trends and to adapt to the changing environment. They can do so on their own, or they can team up with FinTech firms through loose co-operations, strategic alliance or mergers and acquisitions. Yet it is important that asset managers evolve at a higher pace than before. Otherwise the fate of most asset managers is sealed just as it was for the dinosaurs.

PART 7

THE WIDER VALUE CHAIN

CHAPTER 18

A NETWORK OF EXPERTS IS THE FUTURE OF ASSET MANAGEMENT

Anna Schmid

There are three distinct elements in a wealth management relationship that complement each other to form a unique experience: Performance, engagement, and trust. I
believe that traditional asset managers and FinTech firms will have to work together
and jointly form a network of experts to deliver this holistic client experience. This
would make every party involved better off.

IS WHAT CLIENTS WANT ACTUALLY WHAT WEALTH MANAGERS OFFER?

The client experience in wealth management is often very unique for each client,
as hardly any clients have similar needs, plans or assets. Therefore, clients require
a tailor-made wealth management solution. According to Ernst & Young, there
are three distinct elements in a wealth management relationship that complement
each other to form a unique experience for wealth management clients: Performance, engagement, and trust.

Interests between wealth managers and clients are mostly aligned. However,
when it comes to transparency, wealth managers need to improve their disclosure

WealthTech: Wealth and Asset Management in the FinTech Age, pages 121–126.
Copyright © 2020 by Information Age Publishing
121

process significantly. Portfolio performance and fees charged are key drivers of trust to clients. In the past the cost structure has oftentimes not been very transparent and hidden fees were generated for wealth managers through retrocession (e.g. by buying certain high margin products which yielded kickbacks or by receiving trading commissions which incentivized the asset managers to trade more frequently). Transparency helps clients to compare performance net of fees as well as services in general terms and wealth managers will have to adjust to this.

Furthermore, clients increasingly wish to receive information online through digital channels, to which they have access 24/7 from anywhere in the world. Many traditional wealth managers are still lacking this service and therefore may lose clients and revenues. Especially younger generations tend to focus on digital channels, where they can quickly check their account, compare performances, or simply transfer money if need be.

FinTech firms have specialized in looking after these clients' needs. Nowadays new accounts can be opened online within minutes and from anywhere at any time. Some Robo-advisors, for example, only require a new client to answer fewer than ten questions in order to calculate the risk profile and a new account can be opened instantly. The client's personal data is validated via video call that lasts only a few minutes and requires the account opener to hold their ID card to the video camera of the digital device he or she is calling from. This means there is no more need to have lengthy face to face meetings with client advisors. There is no more waiting for the bank's or asset managers' opening hours to have an appointment. Furthermore, the performance generated, and fees charged are shown most transparently on standardized reports which can be downloaded at any time. These high levels of service rendered by FinTech firms have significantly eaten into the pricing power of traditional asset managers, while substantially increasing service expectations of wealth management.

HOW THE ASSET MANAGEMENT INDUSTRY WILL CHANGE WITHIN THE NEXT FEW YEARS

Asset and wealth managers face several difficulties: Capital markets seem to be overvalued by historical standards but nevertheless there is a search for yield. What complicates matters further is that too much money is around to find any bargains. Geopolitical and political risks are unusually high, and the economic growth seems historically weak, given that we are currently experiencing the biggest financial experiment in history thanks to the central banks' ultra-loose monetary policy.

On top of that, asset and wealth managers have often been scrutinized in the past for charging too high a fee (including retrocession or kickbacks) and underperforming their benchmarks. Most importantly, new financial market regulations will come into effect in the European Union with MiFID II in 2018 and the Financial Services Act (FinSA, i.e. the code of conduct with respect to financial services related to financial instruments) in Switzerland. Basically, the regulatory changes in Switzerland with FinSA and the Financial Institutions Act (FinIA), along with the Financial Markets Infrastructures Act (FinfraG), are supposed to ensure that Swiss law is in line with international standards and will be deemed equivalent to MiFID II. The regulatory burdens will substantially increase costs for traditional wealth managers.

One thing that MiFID II requires is that brokers separately invoice trading, research, and advisory going forward. Until now, many asset managers had negotiated all-in-fees with their brokers for these services. Asset managers will then have to rethink which research they truly require and are willing to pay for. Specialized, cutting-edge, alpha generating research will be in demand, while many secondary research providers with a poor or average performance will lose out and may even disappear.

Asset managers who provide standardized, easily scalable, and transparent services to clients have and will be able to acquire significant client assets. Through their standardized offerings, these asset managers can provide their services cheaper, yet, the unique and tailor-made client experience will disappear. A case in point are Robo-advisors, which have highly scalable business models, a low cost-base and highly standardized offerings. Face to face meetings or personal advice is not offered in this context, hence these firms are not able to offer the full holistic wealth management experience that private clients oftentimes wish for.

Asset and wealth managers therefore have to rethink their business models. Switzerland, for example, one of the largest asset management markets in the world, has many so-called independent asset managers (IAMs). According to a study by the Institute of Financial Services Zug IFZ, roughly 2'500 asset managers exist in Switzerland with a median of 2.5 full-time employees, CHF 90m assets under management and a net margin of 0.8%. For these smaller asset managers, remaining independent and marketing their independence from banks, has been the unique selling point in the past. Only by being independent these firms can convincingly demonstrate their "best in class" approach for any product as they have no conflicts of interest as banks do, which regularly prefer to sell their own high margin products. This business model has worked extremely well for the independent asset managers in the past, but the upcoming changes required by law darken their business outlook. With only little resources available, business is getting increasingly difficult for small asset managers. Many firms may not survive the upcoming regulatory changes and many industry experts foresee that the number of asset managers will therefore decline significantly in Switzerland. Some of the independent players in wealth management may merge with others, sell out to larger companies, retire, or simply return funds to investors and close down. Another possibility, and in my view the only one to remain independent and to keep the "best in class" approach, would be to build a network of experts.

To better understand my point of view, let us first have a look at the current business model, where all services are created by the identical entity.

For these—oftentimes very small—IAMs one key to remain independent is to build up an efficient network of experts. This system of interlinked specialists could replace their current "everything under one roof" business model. In this efficient network of experts' business model, IAMs would outsource all services to which they cannot add significant value for the clients.

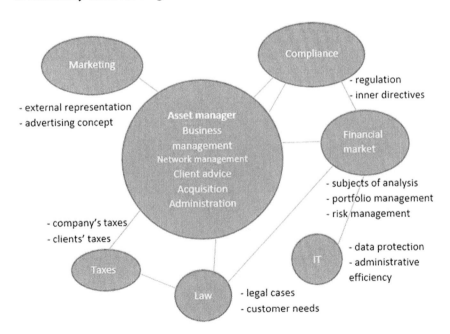

Moreover, outsourcing can also present a way to comply with upcoming regulations as customer care, investment research, decision making, execution, advisory, risk control and compliance may soon be required to be performed by different people. Following an inhouse approach would increase costs for asset managers and eat into their margin. More importantly, for the smaller IAMs with only a median of 2.5 employees, this approach is economically simply is not feasible.

With regards to functions such as legal, compliance and IT shifts towards outsourcing can already be observed. As far as portfolio management, research, and advisory is concerned, however, the trend is just beginning. Although outsourcing portfolio management tasks may seem odd to many industry players at first glance, it may very well make sense for many asset and wealth managers. Asset and wealth managers are first and foremost client relationship managers. Nevertheless, many asset and wealth managers would claim that portfolio management and research which are typically associated with significant costs would constitute for the bulk of their work. Asset and wealth management is a high margin business closely related to the client assets under management. As long as they are sizeable everyone involved gets paid handsomely. However, in times of shrinking assets and increasing costs IAMs need to put more emphasize on cost-efficiency.

One the one hand, outsourcing research, advisory, portfolio management, compliance and IT can significantly reduce overhead costs and reduce personnel risk (e.g. someone falling sick or leaving the company). Most importantly, however, a single person or small team can hardly be an expert in all areas and across all geographic regions. Therefore, outsourcing to true experts can even add credibility to the asset and wealth managers. Outsourcing partners on the other hand can achieve scale effects as they serve several different asset and wealth managers simultaneously. On top of that, these outsourcing partners, too, may need assistance on certain topics and return to potential clients for help. If everyone specializes in what they are best at, everyone is better off. The goal would to make the cake bigger for everyone involved and this can be achieved when everyone specializes in what they are best at and then trades it.

Furthermore, the financial literacy of clients has increased substantially over the past years by the means of digitalization. Handling clients' questions, requests, and complaints becomes more and more time consuming. These requests are often submitted in large quantities at times with high market volatility, i.e. when in-house personnel are particularly preoccupied with running the day-to-day business. I therefore believe that the asset management industry will move towards a network of experts, where not only workloads can be better balanced, but also where the best will thrive in their functions.

CONCLUSION

According to Credit Suisse appr. USD 130 trn. of client assets are being managed by global wealth managers. In 2016 Ernst & Young conducted a study that revealed that 40% of wealth management clients are open to switch their managers and this reveals a USD 175-200bn global revenue opportunity for those companies who are willing to deliver a superior client experience.

Money is no longer as "sticky" as it used to be. Trust and a personal relationship may be important to some clients, especially to those of older generations. For the younger generation, however, transparency, user experience, and performance is more important. Since new accounts can be opened within minutes from anywhere at any time and performance can be easily compared, we expect clients to their switch wealth and asset managers more often. Clients will therefore only be "sticky" if their three requirements are met: performance, engagement, and trust. Whichever IAM provides these qualities will earn substantial revenues in the future.

Due to changed client expectations and to past mishaps in the industry, we expect the industry to change significantly starting in 2018 when MiFID II comes into effect. The best way to comply with the regulatory changes and to meet client expectations, wealth and asset managers ought to connect in networks of experts, where each expert group specializes in one particular skill.

We are glad that FinTechs and Wealthtech firms have entered the market as they have improved transparency significantly. Their digital offerings were a wake-up call to many traditional asset managers who are now forced to evolve. But neither traditional asset managers nor Wealthtech firms offer the "perfect" wealth management experience on their own. Hence, working together as a network of experts could not only make the cake bigger for every stakeholder involved, but firstly result in happier clients. And if clients are happy, this is all we can wish for.

ENDNOTES

1. Ernst & Young. http://www.ey.com/Publication/vwLUAssets/EY-could-your-client-needs-be-your-competitive-advantage/$FILE/EY-could-your-client-needs-be-your-competitive-advantage.pdf
2. Institut für Finanzdienstleistungen Zug IFZ https://www.hslu.ch/en/lucerne-university-of-applied-sciences-and-arts/research/projects/detail/?pid=1095
3. Capra Ibex Investment Partners AG. http://www.caib.ch/business/meinung/meinung-details/vermoegensverwalter.html
4. Outsourcing is key to asset managers independence. http://citywire.ch/news/outsourcing-is-key-to-asset-managers-independence-says-zug-am-adviser/a979449

CHAPTER 19

DECRYPTING THE WEALTHTECH MINDSET

Richard-Marc Lacasse and Berthe Lambert

This text explores the wealth and asset management arena where a new intelligent digital ecosystem is reinventing the rules. The manuscript sheds light on the evolution of the financial sector and expounds on the development of financial technologies, with special attention paid to the various conceptual models related to wealth and asset management. The models describe the FinTech and WealthTech arenas as complex adaptive systems. The authors also investigate the mindset by which WealthTech ventures create, deliver, and capture value—whether such value is economic, social, cultural, or of any other form. Online Wealth Management will be described via case studies. The conclusion explores the future: Symbiosis of traditional institutions with new WealthTech ventures.

PURPOSE STATEMENT AND TERMS

This paper's first challenge is to encapsulate key elements of the WealthTech ecosystem despite the complexity of the sector. A focal point is therefore to demystify the FinTech and WealthTech mindset arenas. The models are original and based on case studies made by the FinTechLab.ca in Canada. Ultimately, this contribution will shed new light on the future of the WealthTech industry. What exactly is WealthTech? Canada's FinTechLab.ca defines it as follows: "Field arising from the symbiosis of digital platforms, Internet of Things (IoT) and artificial intel-

WealthTech: Wealth and Asset Management in the FinTech Age, pages 127–133.

ligence (AI) in wealth and asset management, generally at odds with traditional advisory firms in the sector" (Lacasse & Lambert 2017b). With academic knowledge on WealthTech still relatively limited, we concur with Henry Mintzberg of McGill University, who stated: "It seems far more important to research important topics with soft methodologies than marginal topics with elegant methodologies. (…) Most of the real insight has come from studies that used soft methodologies." (Mintzberg, 1979). An exploratory and qualitative approach was selected because of the constraints of WealthTech's exponential growth, which means that the 2013–2016 database is already obsolete. Although Canada's FinTechLab.ca investigated the phenomenon in the United States, in China and in United Kingdom, most of the fieldwork and action-research were done in Canada. Data sources ranged from classical ethnography to state and governmental studies, documentary evidence, participant observation, semi-structured interviews, action-research and case studies (Wealthsimple, Betterment and Wealthfront). Data from research reports by the Big Four accounting firms (PWC, Deloitte, EY and KPMG) were also very useful.

INTELLIGENT DIGITAL ECOSYSTEM REINVENTING THE RULES

A new intelligent digital ecosystem is reinventing the rules. Geographical limitations no longer matter, and information is relayed in real time. Uganda, Botswana and Ghana communities reinvented microfinance in 2004 via money transfer and mobile wallets; in 2007, Vodaphone's M-Pesa's recuperated the concept in Kenya and Tanzania. In North-America, the millennials are changing transaction patterns. According to the Millennial Disruption Index, 73% of millennials would be more excited about a new offering in financial services from Google, Amazon, Apple, PayPal and Square than from traditional institutions. Business models in every field of activity need to be updated and redesigned. The advent of the Internet of Things (IoT) has brought about an economic tsunami: "Innovations in IoT, which has its roots at MIT, are driving remarkable new technologies and enhancing existing platforms in almost every major industry." (Conner-Simons, 2016). In the world of wealth and asset management, artificial intelligence (AI) is starting to have a major impact on investing and risk management. In some cases, IA plays the role of consultant, interacting directly with the user, with no human interface. A computer algorithm has even been appointed to the board of directors of Deep Knowledge Ventures, a company in Hong Kong. The robot is entitled to vote and supplies series of statistics on subjects discussed by the board. Some USD 30 bn in assets of the largest fund in the world, BlackRock Inc., will rely more on robots rather than humans to make decisions on what to buy and sell. A FinTech startup, R3, founded in 2014, leads a consortium of more than 70 of the world biggest financial institutions in research and development of Blockchain database usage in the financial system.

According to the World Economic Forum, thousands of new ventures are disrupting the traditional financial services sector. An EY Report states that "Fin-

Techs are moving in on the traditional financial services landscape and their products and services are catching on. For traditional services companies, including banks, insurers, wealth and asset management companies, the risk of disruption is real." On the other hand, the Global FinTech Report observes that FinTech and traditional financial services are partnering and "competing less and coming together" (PWC, 2017). Digital deposits, crowdlending and wealth management suggest alternative models, thereby changing the market dynamics of traditional players. In the coming years, online capital raising will transform the role of traditional intermediaries. The empowerment of clients through intelligent systems will also transform the role of investment advisors. Intelligent digital tools will disrupt capital markets and bring about a world where clients and providers will be better connected in real time than ever before. IoT and telematics are also reinventing the value chain of the ever-more-connected insurance and wealth management industry. Traditional financial transactions are on the decline. Agent involvement will become more and more obsolete in the future, and wealth managers need to adapt their computer systems and distribution channels accordingly. Insurance and wealth management are now clashing with a heavily regulated industry that is less and less able to compete with the low operating costs of virtual agents. Some companies have already automated the process of providing advice to customers: asset allocation, management services and tax optimization are all provided online. This democratizes access to financial advice, traditionally a privilege of the wealthy. In response, traditional wealth management funds have adopted similar tactics through Robo-advisors.

EXPLORING THE WEALTHTECH ARENA

Exploratory modelling can be useful to decrypt a new phenomenon. In a collaborative brainstorming exercise on the emergence of FinTech and WealthTech with Dee W. Hock, the FinTechLab.ca identifies the problems to be tackled and the questions that need to be answered. Dee W. Hock is the founder and former CEO of VISA International, a FinTech precursor in the seventies. In addition to his successful career in the financial industry, Hock has been active in developing new models for social and business organizations. He has been particularly interested in forms of organization that are neither rigidly controlled nor anarchic, a hybrid form coined as "chaordic". Hock has authored a book on the subject, Birth of the Chaordic Age (2000) in which he argues that traditional firms are inefficient because their organizations have become too complex. Hock advocates a new organizational form that he qualifies as "chaordic," or simultaneously chaotic and orderly (Figure 19.1). He credits the worldwide fintech success of VISA to its chaordic structure (complex, adaptive, and self-organizing). On January 22 2017, FinTechLab.ca contacted Hock for his insight; he brought the following contribution:

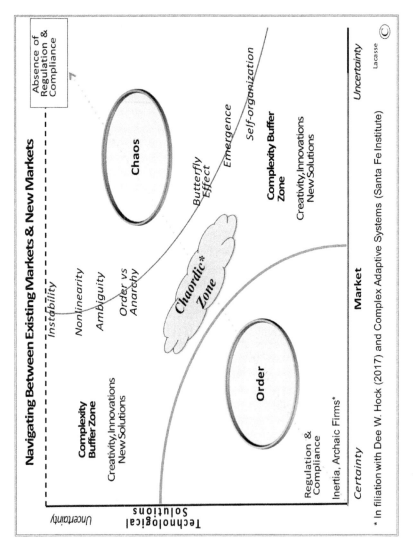

FIGURE 19.1.

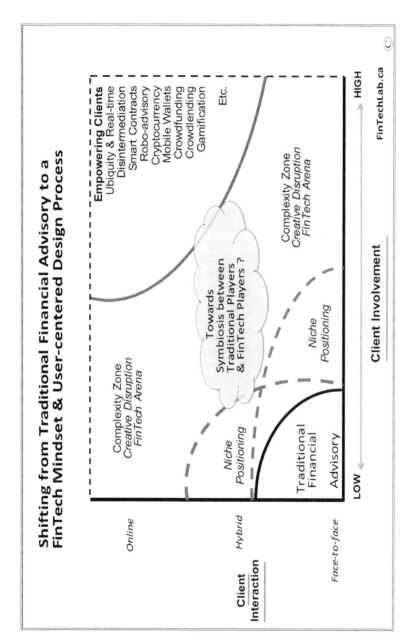

FIGURE 19.2.

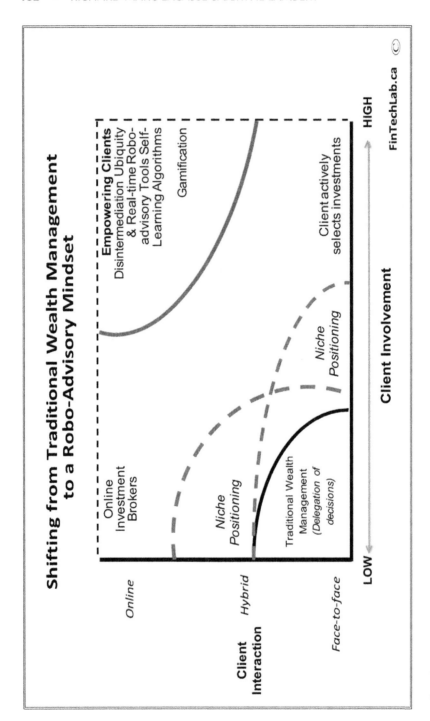

FIGURE 19.3.

The FinTech and WealthTech phenomenon is an evolutional adjustment from over-control toward that ground nature and evolution ever seeks and finds—the harmonious combination of chaos and order, which I coined the word "Chaordic" to describe. One might say the financial service industry is escaping control to come into order. It could overshoot for a time and create some chaos.

Concepts drawn from Complex Adaptative Systems Theory (Santa Fe Institute) also offer new ways to observe the WealthTech phenomenon. The Santa Fe Institute describes the notion of "edge of chaos": healthy, adaptive systems will always exhibit a kind of dynamic tension between chaos and order. Wealth-Tech fits in beautifully with the dynamic tensions observed in the financial service arena: competition and initiative as throughout traditional financial services—"chaos"—while building in mechanisms for cooperation—"order." (see Figure 19.2 and Figure 19.3)

CRACKING THE CODE OF A WEALTHTECH BUSINESS MODEL

A business model describes the means by which a venture creates, delivers, and captures value—whether such value is economic, social, cultural, or of any other form. When a WealthTech venture capitalist manages money, he has an obligation to create value (WealthTech ventures with low profits but having a large online community also has great value). Whatever the model, WealthTech ventures use intelligent online platforms in creative ways as they attempt to craft solutions that are more cost-effective than traditional financial services. They often draw on original activities to generate a better return on investment. WealthTech ventures are inventive regarding cost structures, revenues, and capital requirements.

The FinTechLab.ca Mindset Model consists of interlocking elements that create and deliver value for stakeholders. WealthTech ventures must create a better customer value proposition than traditional financial services. The profitable formula is the blueprint that defines how a WealthTech venture creates value for itself while providing value to customers. It consists of the following formula: revenues often come from very small fees originating from a very large online community. The cost structure is predominantly driven by efficient online platforms, good marketing strategies and « phishing via gamification ». It is important to identify the key resources, which are the assets such as intelligent technology, whiz kids, facilities, venture funds, networks and brands required to deliver the value proposition to the targeted customers. The aim is to effectively interlock the key resources: charismatic leaders, major business sponsors, media, and expertise. Some successful WealthTech ventures, using gamification, design complex operational and managerial processes that allow them to deliver value in such a way as to successfully repeat their activities and increase their revenue and their online community week after week.

REFERENCES

Conner-Simons, A. (2016, Jan 26). *Web inventor teaches web course—Learn about "internet of things"* Retrieved from https://www.csail.mit.edu/iot_professional_education_course_2016.

Mintzberg, H. (1979). Organizational power and goals: A skeletal theory. In D. Schendel & C. Hofer (Eds.), *Strategic management: A new view of business policy and planning* (pp. 64–80). Boston, MA: Little, Brown and Co.

PWC. (2017). *Global FinTech report* (p. 20). London, UK:PWC Global.

CHAPTER 20

CRYPTOASSET PORTFOLIOS

The Next Wave of Digital Asset Management

Floyd DCosta

Cryptocurrencies went through highs and lows over the past years. Oftentimes these boom-and-bust-cycles were further amplified by low liquidity. While there are indeed some efforts by incumbent players to institutionalize digital assets, security token offerings (STOs) have not yet been widely accepted by investors. This contribution discusses the hurdles for mainstream adoption of crypto assets and how these hurdles could be mastered in the near future.

While cryptocurrencies had a rollercoaster year swinging wildly from all-time highs to fresh new lows, 2018 also was the year when new cryptoassets emerged and started to gain increasing attention among investors and participants. Over the past twelve months, the markets saw a fresh new wave of entrants—security token offering (STO) platforms, stablecoins and even established financial institutions took the plunge. From Nasdaq and Fidelity to the Gibraltar Stock Exchange and SIX Swiss Exchange, leading institutions entered the world of digital assets, announcing a variety of crypto related products and services. Separately, a recent research by Bitwise and ETF Trends revealed that around 79% of financial advisors received queries from their clients on cryptoassets and 22% of them were planning to start new allocation into such assets or expand their existing cryptoasset portfolio. However, despite increasing interest and curiosity, cryptoassets continue to remain in the fringe and have yet to gain acceptance as a standard investment avenue.

WealthTech: Wealth and Asset Management in the FinTech Age, pages 135–138.
Copyright © 2020 by Information Age Publishing
All rights of reproduction in any form reserved.

WHAT'S HOLDING BACK MAINSTREAM ADOPTION?

One of the biggest impediments to mainstream adoption of cryptoassets is the lack of clear regulations and laws governing their usage. While some governments have put in place regulations that define the scope of cryptocurrencies and their trading, it continues to vary wildly, with multiple jurisdictions worldwide refusing to recognize them as legitimate instruments of trade and currency.

However, even as regulators continue to understand and refine regulations, the absence of structured product offerings to engage in and trade such digital assets have also kept investors at bay. Conventional markets have indices, mutual funds and structured products that investors find easy to invest in and love trading with. However, the crypto world is only just getting started and is still restricted to primary assets. As a result, leading financial institutions like banks, hedge funds, family offices and even private investors remain hesitant to dip their toe into the emerging world of crypto.

Separately, the lack of custodial services—the secure and legal holding of the digital assets, along with limited liquidity also adds to the lack of confidence among investors.

HOW TO BRING CRYPTOASSETS INTO THE MAINSTREAM

There is a definite need for innovation—new platforms, new models—that blend together the familiar traditional finance product structures with emerging digital assets classes to create cryptoasset-based structured investment products. These need to be easily accessible and convenient for investors to invest into and trade. To get started, various primary cryptoassets issued in the form of tokens can be curated and packaged to create ready-to-invest portfolios, which can then be bought and traded via emerging digital exchanges.

A set of tokens of tokens can be selected by experts and fund managers based on certain themes and related criteria. These can then be bundled using smart contracts and offered to investors as familiar structured products. The entire set can then be managed and traded OTC as well as via centralized and decentralized digital asset exchanges. A number of protocols have evolved over 2018 that allow for the bundling, management and unbundling of a basket of tokens. More popular ones include the SET protocol and the Basket protocol. This, in turn, has led to the emergence of platforms that allow for the seamless curation, management and trading of token baskets using smart contracts.

Platforms like Tokenomatic, a decentralized Digital Asset Management platform, enable the creation, distribution and management of a composite basket of tokens, thereby allowing investors to instantly access, buy and trade an expert-curated portfolio of cryptoassets; all powered by self-executing smart contracts.

HOW IT ALL COMES TOGETHER

On the platform, experts, including fund managers and other licensed entities can curate tokens, structure theme-based portfolios and create multiple crypto prod-

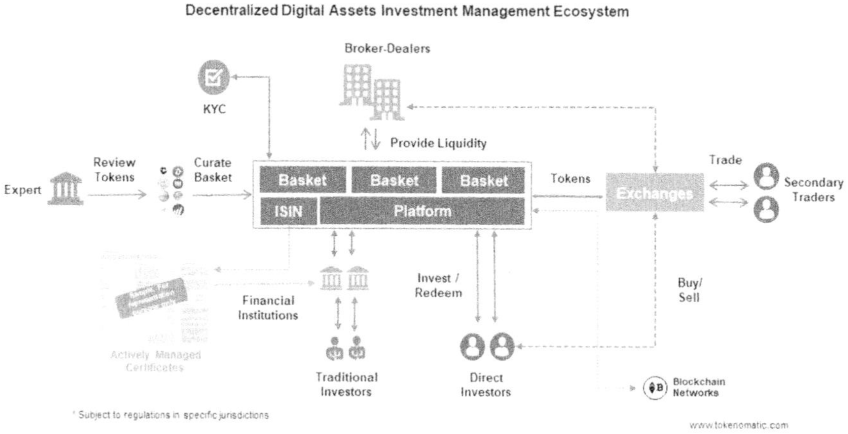

Decentralized Digital Assets Investment Management Ecosystem

FIGURE 20.1.

ucts that offer varying risk levels and returns on investment. Individuals and financial institutions looking to invest can explore various such cryptoasset product offerings and request for one of more of such offerings. Dealers receive and fulfil buy/sell requests from investors while also acting as liquidity providers.

Investors receive ownership of their cryptoasset product in the form of tokens, based on the amount invested. They can then choose to trade these tokens on digital exchanges, redeem them to claim their share of the underlying cryptoassets (where offered) or simply redeem them for fiat currency. The entire underlying portfolio is held in custody by the smart contract itself on behalf of the investors in a transparent and cryptographically secure manner.

The emergence of credible stablecoins has helped smoothen the transition between fiat and the token economy; thereby allowing for a variety of participants to actively engage in such a marketplace. Additionally, using Actively Managed Certificates, an ISIN code can be created for each basket thereby also allowing bank wealth managers and licensed financial advisors to access and offer the product to their clients.

WHERE DO WE GO FROM HERE?

While the regulations gradually come around in the various jurisdictions, the emergence of structured products will definitely help bring cryptoassets into the mainstream. Blending familiar traditional finance product structures with emerging digital models to create cryptoasset-based structured offerings will allow investors to invest and trade in ways they are already familiar with, balance holdings and smartly manage risk.

Empowering various licensed entities to participate in the cryptoasset markets will address the liquidity issue, while leveraging smart contracts for custody of the assets will mitigate transparency and security concerns.

Today, the opportunity exists for financial institutions and startups alike to craft integrated digital asset management platforms that will allow for the creation of the next generation of financial marketplaces; inclusive, efficient and transparent, powered by Blockchain technology. These will seamlessly bring together various market participants—incumbents and new ones, elevate crypto trade and effectively enable the digital transformation of the asset management industry as a whole.

As more financial institutions begin trading and investing in cryptoassets, as well as begin to offer such products to their customers, it will not only help legitimize such financial products by urging authorities to implement regulations to manage them, but will also help foster their mainstream adoption as a credible financial asset worth investing in.

PART 8

PRODUCT DEVELOPMENT AND INNOVATION

CHAPTER 21

HOW WEALTHTECH IS RE-INVENTING THE CUSTOMER EXPERIENCE BY LINKING OPEN INNOVATION AND TECHNOLOGY

Daniel Fasnacht

Open innovation is the prerequisite on which new technology can be built on. It has triggered a boom in the FinTech industry—not only in the Silicon Valley but also in New York, London Switzerland, and Asia. Around USD 50 bn have been invested in FinTech startups worldwide by business angels, venture capital and, private equity firms since the financial crisis.

Having understood WealthTech as described in this book, we are explaining in this section that an open approach towards innovation is the prerequisite for success. In other words, it was open innovation that delivered the foundation on which technological developments were built. These developments then evolved and fundamentally changed customer experiences, leading to the creating of significant customer value. But FinTech should do more than simply supporting electronic trading and payments or moving assets faster at lower cost. Using new

WealthTech: Wealth and Asset Management in the FinTech Age, pages 141–146.
Copyright © 2020 by Information Age Publishing
All rights of reproduction in any form reserved.

technology to appeal to certain client segments is a step forward but definitely not enough. If we furnish millennials with easy to use tools for investing and managing their wealth, the industry as such will not grow, instead, we merely provide some financial wellness platforms to an increasingly sophisticated clientele. As in all innovation cycles before, startups as well as established large multinationals must serve ever changing customer needs—not as an end in itself, but with the overall objective in mind to make money.

ADAPTING OPEN INNOVATION TO THE WEALTH AND ASSET MANAGEMENT INDUSTRY

Many components aiming to improve the customer experience have been developed by smart and innovative firms over the last years. Some even found effective ways to integrate their services or apps into the value chains of wealth or asset management. The lubricant, however, to make all these efforts profitable is open innovation. The real economy acknowledged this new imperative for creating and profiting from technology explained in the book "Open Innovation" by Henry Chesbrough (2003) nearly two decades ago. Yet, it needed some time until members of the financial services industry also acknowledged that they can better serve their customers by opening up innovation processes and business models (Fasnacht, 2009). The Open Innovation paradigm is in stark contrast to the traditional (closed) innovation paradigm of offering exclusively proprietary products and services and managing the entire investment process internally. Nowadays, institutional investors as well as retail clients do not care any longer where an investment service or mutual fund originated. Instead, they consider to what level this product or service corresponds to their risk and investment profile as well as investment portfolios and how it fits with other aspects of their lives as well as asset classes.

Evidently, on the one hand customers forced wealth and asset managers to provide access to products and services beyond their organization's own business model (outside-in). On the other hand, clients also pushed wealth and asset managers down a path where internal ideas are allowed to permeate through organizational boundaries and to venture to other companies for use in their business and distribution models (inside-out).

INSIDE-OUT OFFERS BEST OF BREED FUND SELECTION

Open innovation has prevailed within the asset management industry under the label of open or guided architecture. It became common practice for sophisticated clients to pick their favored funds from the global fund universe, regardless of where they have their custody account or domicile. This explains not only the rise of some funds on a global scale in terms of assets under management but also the power these funds obtained through their investments in stock- exchange listed companies. From a client's perspective, the open fund architecture enables unbiased investment advice and overall improves asset allocation and diversification. Client advisors can select financial products ideally suited to their client's needs, investment and risk profile, irrespective of where they are produced—in-house or by a third-party provider. Apparently, this fosters an environment of transparency with growing trust between client and advisor. Thus, the client finally arrived at the center of the investment process a result that is furthermore highlighted by all the recent client centricity projects across major financial institutes.

For vendors, this change offered new distribution channels. There is hardly any asset manager left who does not promote its internally managed fund to other asset managers in order for them to sell it to their clients too. That is exactly where FinTech startups jump in: embracing Open Innovation and building up solutions utilizing latest technology. In consequence, many fund marketplaces and platforms evolved. Asset managers broke with the traditional (closed) product development and distribution process and now collaborate with one another while also competing with each other. But there are also proprietary global platforms for third party funds, offering access to hundreds of fund providers and distribution partners. Market leaders such as Allfunds Bank with CHF 260bn under management and UBS Fondcenter with CHF 190 bn strive for economies of scale where size and volume is everything. While fees came under pressure because kick-back fees have been banned, tighter regulations such as MiFID II made platform operations even more expensive. Emerging platform providers are forced to offer something special to their investors. This niche was seized by a FinTech from Switzerland that services the end-to-end hedge fund investment cycle with easy access and entirely online. Fundbase pursues two avenues: alternative investment analysts provide added value by identifying high-quality managers early on, before they lose their edge. Secondly, it computes community driven data by advanced machine learning algorithms, enabling investors to make decisions that they could otherwise not consistently make at scale.

Whereas the concept of open innovation laid the foundation for open architecture in the funds industry with platforms that have grown vastly over the last ten years, it is now at the discretion of investors, on how they assess these niche-player platforms.

OUTSIDE-IN PROMOTES WHITE LABEL SERVICES

The outside-in Open Innovation approach, in contrast to inside-out process, focuses on customer needs rather than product platforms. An organization driven by an outside-in culture is constantly looking for ways to expand demand. This may answer the question on how to practically create additional customer value. If business development and value propositions derive from market research and field studies this model should prevail. Given the outside-in Open Innovation approach and the corresponding usage of technology, white labelling is one possibility to create value for customers. Investopedia explains a white label product or service as something that is manufactured by one company and packaged and distributed by another company under various brand names. First implementations began more than 30 years ago in the CD and DVD sector and became increasingly popular in the financial services industry about ten years ago. Asset managers embraced the opportunity to shorten research and product development cycles by insourcing external products and services. UBS as one of the first banks to offer white labelling solutions for traditional and alternative fund structures, while many other asset manager recently integrated external investment strategies into their solution portfolio.

The customer-centric view and technological advancements such as mobile and cloud computing and social media finally redefined traditional innovation models and accelerated the outside-in approach of Open Innovation. Without further elaborating on the digital advice market and systematic wealth management through exchange traded funds, Robo-advisors are predestined as white label solutions.

Deutsche Bank Asset Management and the Swiss insurance company Baloise announced in July 2017 to collaborate on the usage of a new investment robot. "WISE" stands for White label Investment Software Engine and was designed by the FinTech division of Deutsche Asset Management. The Swiss insurer will provide the tailor-made investment solutions produced by the Robo-advisor mainly to European retail clients under the brand name of Baloise Monviso. The strategy of making technology available to third party providers as a white-label solution may change traditional value chains, affecting producers, suppliers, and advisors alike. Distributing solutions to the client through a business-to-business-to-customer arrangement (B2B2C) might be the beginning of a new era in the digitization process of the banking industry (Deutsche Bank, 2017).

On the other hand, the bank signed a partnership agreement with a Swiss FinTech, Descartes Finance, as a client for its ETF strategy portfolios. Through this form of outside-in, Descartes Finance gets access to the knowledge of the global research and analysis of the Deutsche Asset Management. Affluent clients can benefit from currently six actively managed portfolios provided through Descartes Finances' discretionary mandates over its online platform. Yet, is has to be highlighted that such emerging B2B2C business models can only work if the value adding processes are aligned to platform technology, including digital onboarding, risk management and portfolio reporting.

HOW TO MAKE THE BEST OF ALL

Regardless of which one of the two alternatives of Open Innovation—*outside-in* or *inside-out* dominates businesses—overall, we can say that latest applications do rarely follow the one or the other approach. Employing both and collaborating with complementary firms is what Gassmann and Enkel (2004) described as third open innovation approach as the *coupled process.* If the focus is on learning from customers while implementing the coupled process with digital platforms, we come close to disruptive business models that have the power to completely change the customer experience as a can been seen from the multiple variations of crowdfunding, i.e. crowd-donating, crowd-lending, crowd-investing and recently crowd-equity. Even though the phenomenon of crowdfunding is older than the term itself, one of the earliest definitions of the concept clearly relates to openness, collaboration and digitalization. *"If these truly are the "creators of tomorrow," then the aesthetic of tomorrow is collaboration and open-source creativity. Nowhere is this clearer than in the work of Hanson, a noted author, filmmaker and "film futurist" whose latest project, A Swarm of Angels, is a crowdfunded, open-source feature film that will be made collaboratively with an international community of online participants."* (Shatkin, 2007).

Most varieties of crowdfunding are a combination of the inside-out and outside-in approach, extended by the customer demand to find and close deals on a digital platform. This platform is called a peer-to-peer (P2P) market and is estimated to be worth globally over USD 200bn according to international research sources. Swiss studies forecast an exponential growth for sums raised in the crowdfunding market over the next years (Dietrich & Amrein, 2017). The fastest growing segment is crowdlending for real estate that applies debt financing, allowing people to borrow and lend money online. Interestingly, in Switzerland, real estate crowd-lending makes up 25% of the total crowd-investing market. In the USA only 1.3% go into property financing, little more in the UK with 2.7%, Germany 3.2% or France 4%. It is the regulatory environment that exerts considerable influence on the development of this new industry although it is clear that property can be financed easier, cheaper, and online without a bank. The biggest P2P platform is Lending Club, founded in the US in 2017 that reached over USD 20bn in loans and 45% market share. In Switzerland, the market is much smaller, but when looking at emerging P2P platforms, the dynamics of further growth become evident. There is increasing competition among players, bringing together capital providers and investors for real estate. While acting as virtual intermediaries, some emerging startups may have the power to disrupt the traditional mortgage lending market which is today dominated by banks.

CONCLUSION

Whether it is open fund architecture, white labelling solutions or P2P platforms, whether it refers to just a few possible applications that link open innovation and technology or and an entire range, it is the sum of exploited ideas and newly created products, services, and platforms that will add customer value. The new WealthTech imperatives will be full transparency, accessibility, autonomy, comfort, and costs. As a result, clients will get empowered not just to invest, borrow, or bank, but to completely change their behaviour regarding all of their financial matters. In view of available online platforms people are ever less inclined to step through the doors of a bank or credit institution. As new rules will follow new client habits, many established firms need to do more than just focus on how to optimize their core business. Together with FinTech firms that are seeking disruption, wealth managers must fully align their innovation activities to leverage the benefits of digitalization. Soon we will see additional concepts beyond Open Innovation towards innovation ecosystems that will have the power to change the wealth management business model.

REFERENCES

Chesbrough, H. (2003). *Open innovation: The new imperative for creating and profiting from technology.* Boston, MA: Harvard Business School Press.

Deutsche Bank. (2017). *Enjoy investing—Deutsche Asset Management adds first partner to WISE Robo platform.* Retrieved from: https://www.db.com/newsroom_news/2017/ghp/enjoy-investing-deutsche-asset-management-adds-first-partner-to-wise-robo-platform-en-11582.htm, *4 July 2017.*

Dietrich, A., & Amrein, S. (2017). *Crowdfunding monitoring Switzerland 2017.* Zug: Institute of Financial Services Zug IFZ.

Fasnacht, D. (2009). *Open innovation in the financial services: Growing through openness, flexibility and customer integration.* Berlin/Heidelberg: Springer.

Gassmann, O., & Enkel, E. (2004). *Towards a theory of open innovation: Three core process archetypes.* Paper presented at the R&D Management Conference (RADMA), Lisbon, Portugal, 7 July 2004.

Shatkin, E. (2007). *Remixing & crowdsourcing: Creators series showcases the aesthetic of the new millennium.* Retrieved from: https://laist.com/2007/06/15/remixing_crowds.php

CHAPTER 22

VENTURE CAPITAL AND BANKS INVESTING IN STARTUPS VIA CORPORATE VENTURE CAPITAL

Maurizio Ballesteros and Felix Cardenas

Banking is in need of disruption; the current product and services offering is not meeting the users' needs adequately. Waiting times, paperwork, and transactions that require physical interaction are still activities that are practiced across markets and financial institutions. The best alternative to disrupt the banking industry is to look at innovation from an Open Innovation approach.

Open innovation strategies have proved to be helpful and successful in technology sectors and companies such as Google, Apple, Facebook, and Microsoft, so why not apply this Open Innovation approach to banking? This entitles the possibility of large established banks to invest in FinTech startups. FinTech Startups raised USD 2.7bn in 226 deals in the first quarter 2017. Although is figure is impressive, in reality there is a decline of invested dollars to venture capital (VC) backed Fin-Tech startups in 2017. At the current rate it is estimated to have an 18% drop from 2016. There are 22 FinTech startup unicorns[1] valued at USD 77bn. In the U.S., a

---

[1] A unicorn is a startup company valued at over USD 1bn.

WealthTech: Wealth and Asset Management in the FinTech Age, pages 147–150.
Copyright © 2020 by Information Age Publishing
147

startup named SoFi, raised USD 500 m at a USD 4.5 bn valuation, while in China, Rapid Finance, valued at USD 1bn filed for IPO in the first quarter 2017.

LARGE ESTABLISHED BANKS INVESTING THROUGH CORPORATE VENTURE CAPITAL

Corporate venture capital (CVC) is a subset of venture capital wherein corporations make systematic investments into startup companies, often by taking an equity stake in an innovative firm tangentially related to the company's own industry. They often also provide marketing expertise, management, strategic direction, and financial support. During the first quarter 2017, in the FinTech space, corporates participated in nearly a third of every startup investment transaction. This is a dramatic increase of 22% compared with the same period in 2016. More financial services established banks continue to initiate corporate venture capital investment vehicles. Among the top CVC investors there is: Banco Santander InnoVentures, Goldman Sachs, Citigroup, Mizuho Financial Group, JPMorgan Chase, Sumitomo Mitsui Financial Group, Wells Fargo, UBS AG, HSBC, PNC Financial Services, BBVA, ING Group, Capital One, Bank of China, and BNP Paribas. Santander, Goldman Sachs, and Citi have participated in the highest number of deals to finance FinTech startups. The most significant deals in Latin America occurred in Brazil, indicative deals include:

StartUp and Round	Country	Select investors
NU Bank USD 80m (Series D // Q4'16)	Brazil	Founders Fund, KaszekVentures, Sequoia Capital, Tiger Global
NU Bank USD 52m (Series C // Q1'16)	Brazil	Founders Fund, KaszekVentures, Sequoia Capital, Tiger Global
Creditas USD 19.4m (Series B // Q1'17)	Brazil	IFC, KaszekVentures, Naspers, QED Investors, QuonaCapital, Redpointe.ventures
GuiaBolso USD 17.3m (Series C // Q2'16)	Brazil	IFC, KaszekVentures, QED Investors, Ribbit Capital

In Latin America, Brazil had the largest number of startup investment deals with 230, followed by Mexico with 180. Colombia with 84 deals, Argentina with 72, and Chile with 65. These five countries accounted for 90% of the FinTech activity in Latin America. In Mexico, in terms of geographic concentration, 66% of FinTech startups originated in Mexico City, followed by Guadalajara with 11%, and Monterrey with 9%.

FINTECH ECOSYSTEM IN MEXICO

Accelerators and incubators must work closely with financial institutions and venture capital firms. Even though there is a great deal of talent and business ideas in Mexico, the execution is still a big challenge for all. Angel investors and venture capital firms and other players in the market are betting on more mature startups, and there is scarcity of this maturity stage of startups in the Mexican market. Therefore, the involvement of well-designed and effective acceleration programs will help the ecosystem grow. Since 2014, the Mexican FinTech ecosystem has been strengthened due to alternative events fostering FinTech entrepreneurship, including launching incubator and accelerator programs, and completing rounds of capital in Series A and beyond. Examples of these startups are: Konfio, Conekta, Kubo, Kueski and Clip. There is also the 'FinTech Law' proposal promoted by the Secretariat of Treasury and Public Credit. There has also been specialized FinTech conferences like FINNOSUMMIT. These activities support a growing ecosystem in Mexico around FinTech. New players, such as Corporates are entering the picture along with angel investors, new venture capital firms as well as accelerators and incubators. For example, during 2017 a FinTech focused acceleration program managed by Startup bootcamp was created thanks to a collaboration of several financial services institutions. This collaboration included: BanRegio, a regional bank in Mexico, Fiinlab, the innovation arm of Gentera Bank, IGNIA, a venture capital firm, White & Case, a corporate law firm, HSBC, VISA, and Ernst & Young. These institutions came together with one sole purpose in mind, to support the FinTech ecosystem in Mexico. The program supports 11 FinTech startups in different stages of development, each of which are in the process of creating companies with disruptive innovative services. The startups cover several areas in the financial services world. From payment platforms to wealth management and invoice-based lending, these startups are committing to revolutionizing the market. The involvement of the previously mentioned sponsors consist in funding the acceleration program and working actively alongside the entrepreneurs in order to exchange expertise. The sponsors benefit from the innovation and technology these startups are developing as well as their culture, lean operations and agility to react to market needs. On the other side, startups benefit from the market, operations, and the services and products the sponsors currently offer. This win-win relationship is being replicated by other segments and players in the market, thus making a more fertile territory for innovation and startup creation.

Venture capital firms have played a key role in supporting this ecosystem. They are a great means of connecting capital and expertise with startups. In essence, they are merging the gap between investors and entrepreneurs. The newest addition to the investor role are Corporate´s CVC investing units. In the FinTech space, there are some banks in Mexico that are implementing such CVC strategies. BanRegio, for example, just as other banks, is looking to innovate in financial services provided to new and current clients. There is a whole new wave of platforms, applications, algorithms and solutions that make companies' and individuals' life easier by solving their problems in an easy, intuitive way while facilitating a much more enhanced user experience. To achieve this perilous task, BanRegio sees its active involvement in this ecosystem as paramount. Their initial efforts to achieve this have been through sponsoring programs such as Startup bootcamp in collaboration with other key players in the market. Its CVC branch recently announced investment in four key venture capital funds in Mexico that have investment in leading startups in different industries, including FinTech. BanRegio is also doing direct investments in FinTech startups that offer strategic value for their product offering. Alongside these outbound efforts, it is also investing in its internal structure towards more flexibility and agility in order to integrate these technologies into its current structure and market. BanRegioLabs is a division within BanRegio that is also developing new solutions for the market and integrating existing ones.

In addition to looking to sponsor startups and VC funds to innovate, BanRegio wants to propel the startup ecosystem. Its strategy is the creation of a banking division exclusively for startups and entrepreneurs. This segment is underserved and barely banked as their structure and lack of track record alienates them from the current financial services offering of banks and financial institutions. Current bank credit policies and regulations are not able to service the needs and requirements of startups. BanRegio aims to achieve what Silicon Valley Bank or Square One Bank in the USA have achieved. These institutions have innovated their financial services offerings in order to cater their services to this new market, as they know this market is growing and is key for the future. This CVC practice has been done for many years in other countries, which has engaged in a virtuous cycle socially and economically. Mexico, however, is still in the early stages of these activities and has a long road ahead to achieve what has been done in the USA and Europe. There is yet to be more public and resoundingly successful cases from which to learn and set an example for many other companies in Mexico to follow suit.

RESOURCES

CBInsights. (2017, April). *The Global FinTech Report: Q1.* Retrieved from: https://www. cbinsights.com/research/report/fintech-trends-q1-2017/

Andrade, G., Fontao, A., Pombo, C., Morelos, E., Pleguezelos, J., & Goulart, J. (2017, May). *FINTECH: Innovations you may not know were from Latin America and the Caribbean* (pp. 77-80). Inter-American Development Bank and Finnovista.

Dib, D., Ramírez, J., & Alvarado, G. (2017, February). *Panorama del FinTech en Mexico.* Mexico City, NM: Fiinlab Endeavor. Retrieved from: http://www.crowdfunding-mexico.mx/uploads/8/7/7/2/87720184/panorama_fintech_mexico.pdf

IOSCO. (2017, February). *Research report on financial technologies FinTech.* Retrieved from: https://www.thenational.ae/business/markets/market-analysis-mexico-leads-the-pack-among-emerging-markets-1.156302

PART 9

MARKETING AND SALES

CHAPTER 23

DIGITAL FAMILY OFFICE 2.0

Steffen Bassler

Digitization has transformed much of the financial services industry over the past several years, yet family offices have remained largely on the sidelines. There are legitimate reasons for their hesitancy thus far. However, the shift to digitization is inevitable, and it will transform the industry in the coming decade. Those firms which develop a coherent plan for digitization will give themselves a head-start in capitalizing on the advantages of digitization which include stronger client relationships, reduced operating costs, and enhanced risk management and regulatory compliance capabilities.

Family offices come mostly in two categories: single-family office (SFO) or multi-family office (MFO). These types of investment groups are family-controlled, and SFOs are the predominant form of these businesses. Family offices—which have historically operated in highly fragmented and secretive silos—have come under mounting pressure to leverage new technology as newer players including large retail banks expanding their wealth management services enter the fray. While national financial regulators are placing more pressure on increasing transaction transparency, the coming of age of highly technologically savvy third-generation scions of ultra-high-net-worth families means that adopting innovative technology has taken center stage. This new generation of clients demands more accessible services online and pose a strategic challenge to wealth managers.

WealthTech: Wealth and Asset Management in the FinTech Age, pages 153–156.
Copyright © 2020 by Information Age Publishing
All rights of reproduction in any form reserved.

The adoption of innovative wealth management software has historically been slow and asset managers still have a long way to go to recognize and exploit big data and conduct data analytics. This is largely due to a growing compliance burden and a patchwork of legacy systems that distract firms from building new platforms that are critical for serving the next generation of customers. Some firms find it difficult to justify the cost of such IT infrastructure, while others struggle to identify a system with functions and features that match their requirements.

Despite the industry's historical challenges, late adopters playing catch-up have begun working towards addressing the IT requirements for their digital asset management systems. Some firms have adopted social media as a tool to engage with their clients while others have increasingly looked at new strategies of harnessing 'big data' and levering its analytical capabilities to innovate their product offering. Yet others have developed customized platforms and security software to bolster their clients' security systems, as well as improve their client experience.

Faced with mounting competition from newer entrants with cutting-edge data and digital strategies, legacy players are ramping-up their search for customized tools. They not only work to develop technologies to better target younger clients, they also attempt to bolster loyalty from among their long-standing customers. While much software is designed and adopted for generic and functional purposes, family offices are typically driven by individuals that require custom-fit systems which are tailored to the specific needs of a family or group of families. Demand among third-generation clients for customized software platforms is growing rapidly with many family offices spending more than of USD 400,000 on IT infrastructure, and families with more than USD 1 billion in assets spending more than USD 1 million.

Much IT expenditure by family offices has been focused on harnessing big data to solve reporting issues. Indeed, a growing number of firms have worked to aggregate vast amounts of data—on hard assets, real estate securities and private equity investments—on a software-as-a-service (SaaS)-based reporting platform, to actively monitor and manage their exposure.

The decision by family offices to harness big data as a way of enhancing their reporting systems is largely down to the fact that technology becomes critical in mitigating associated risks. This is all the more important as their investments become increasingly complex and diversified, oftentimes across multiple managers and jurisdictions. Therefore, more sophisticated tools for aggregating data have established reporting tools as the 'holy grail' of wealth management technology, not least due to increasing levels of regulation, more complex portfolio requirements and the growing need for clients to access consolidated reports online and in real time.

At the same time, however, greater adoption of these SaaS-based reporting platforms and other classes of technology comes with stark implications about data security online. The complexity of cyber security risks is not well understood by the sector and in many countermeasures to avoid security breaches "starts and finishes with antivirus software". Additionally, breaches through mobile devices, amid developments in the "easily overlooked" Internet of things, have wide-reaching personal safety implications. As family offices customize their offerings and navigate the challenges of a newly digitalized landscape, the use of data and technology will play an increasingly crucial role in allowing firms to both mini-mize competitive gaps and differentiate their services from others.

The aim, as always, should be continuous improvement. And as family offices implement better governance and controls, they will absolutely grow more suc-cessful in the investment realm and will have better processes in place to stream-line communication among various stakeholders and consequently will be able to reach decisions more quickly.

Naturally, family offices do not have the same urgency to deploy capital as fast as other financial sponsors do. Decisions can take longer—sometimes too long. At times family offices lose deals not because they do not have the capital required but because they do not have the process in place to make decisions fast enough. The adoption of technology tools such as online collaboration systems can accel-erate the communication process among family members and lead to better, more rapid decision making.

To compete in the years ahead family offices will need to embrace change. As the speed of business continues to increase, a culture of innovation will be a key differentiator for those family offices that succeed, helping them hasten their growth, improve acquisition strategies, and drive value creation. Leading family offices will understand that gains in the years ahead will depend on how well they can innovate to meet and beat the demands of an increasingly competitive market.

So how does this happen? A critical part of any innovation strategy is the abil-ity to leverage business intelligence and advanced analytics. Not only can a robust data analytics program help a family office drive competitive advantage, it can enable quicker and better decisions on potential investments and uncover profit-generating opportunities within portfolio companies. Moreover, it accelerate the due diligence process and discern market trends that facilitate a profitable, long-term wealth-compounding strategy.

By making better use of data, family offices can analyze and uncover piv-otal market movements and become true strategic partners with their portfolio companies. Ideally, family offices should maintain a management dashboard that consolidates data across all investments. Imagine being able to look across your entire investment portfolio and quickly uncover ways to drive better efficiencies and savings.

As any family office grows, it should continue to search for new ways to drive ever-higher returns. And one of the best ways to do that is by participating in direct investments. After all, many family offices today are eagerly embracing the challenges and responsibilities they once entrusted private equity firms with. Why? Because they understand that direct investments will remain one of the most exciting and rewarding opportunities for the years to come. But there are also ramifications beyond the increased competition with private equity firms: family offices now invest less in in private funds as they prefer direct deals. In short, they do not like being limited partners in private equity funds any longer, because of their preference to invest directly.

Through WealthTech family offices will be able to experience the type of improvements in wealth management that we have seen in other industries who have used digital technology to create whole new business models, along the lines of Uber, Airbnb, Netflix, Expedia, etc. Imagine a family office where every financial and legal advisor is connected with the family by a single phone call. No more spending time and money navigating today's maze of multiple accounting, financial and legal advisors in order to seek advice and purchase financial products. Imagine a financial system where all the information a family needs to make important financial decisions is available right at their fingertips. No more lost or hard to find documents or information that is not readily available.

Modern information and communications technology, powered by digital technologies, enables new service models to be created. Models that will provide every family with a digital family office so they can experience personal wealth management in the digital age.

CHAPTER 24

STRATEGIZING ABOUT ROBO-ADVISE

Claude Diderich

When talking about the future of WealthTech, the buzzword Robo-advise is not far away. But what is Robo-advise? In this section I will review different strategies implemented by Robo-advisors worldwide. I will focus on identifying key challenges and illustrate opportunities for competitive advantage, focusing on desirability, feasibility, and viability.

INTRODUCTION

The financial technology (FinTech) industry has steadily gained attention in recent years. It has grown from being a USD 2.54bn industry in the entire year 2012 to a USD 6.3bn industry in only Q1 of 2019, as measured by venture capitalists backed financing data from CB Insights (2019). One of the key offerings associated with FinTech, especially in the area of wealth management (WealthTech), are Robo-advisors. Different categories of Robo-advisors exist, those that focus on the "robo" part (technology) and those that are more inclined toward the "advice" part (investment strategy). In the former category, are solutions like Scalable Capital or Financial Guard, which define their value proposition through automatic portfolio rebalancing, tax loss harvesting, and dividend reinvestment. The more investment strategy-inclined Robo-advisors tend to focus on understanding

WealthTech: Wealth and Asset Management in the FinTech Age, pages 157–164.

the customer's investment objectives and risk preferences. They offer diversified, strategic asset allocations using ETFs, often relying on goal-based planning, automatic portfolio implementation, and cash management as their main value-added services. Betterment, SigFig, and Wealthsimple fall into this more customer-centric segment of Robo-advisors.

Although different Robo-advisors exhibit different properties and offer unique customer values, they all have the following three characteristics in common:

1. They replace the human interaction with the customer (i.e. the investor) with a *technology-based user interface or user experience*, through web-based interfaces, apps, natural language-recognition systems, or physical robots.
2. They offer some sort of strategic and/or tactical *investment advice based on algorithms*, partially relying on customer or investment strategy expert input; the judgmental aspect of investing is replaced by a systematic and, more often than not, rational approach.
3. They implement an *automatic process for adjusting portfolio holdings* based on the investment advice, automatically generating and executing trades, guaranteeing the best execution.

Developing a successful strategy for a Robo-advise WealthTech firm requires navigating through these different characteristics to design a strategy that is, as Brown (2009) advocates:

a. *desirable*—customers prefer the offering over that from traditional investment advisors and other Robo-advisors;
b. *feasible*—the offering delivers upon the promises made, with respect to investment performance, risk, and costs; and
c. *viable*—customers see value in the offering and are willing to pay a fee that exceeds its manufacturing costs, including running costs, investment amortization, and capital costs.

THREE PERSPECTIVES

There are three different perspectives to approach the development of a Robo-advise strategy.

1. Private Bank Perspective

Many private banks, especially in the current low-interest-rate environment, have a hard time profitably servicing the low-end customer segments, those with less than USD 1mn. in bankable assets. A Robo-advise-based offering may help these banks regain profitability in such customer segments, by reducing costs through replacing expensive human resources with less expensive technology.

Two key challenges nevertheless present themselves. First, asset size is not necessarily a solid customer-segmentation approach to offering Robo-advise. Second, servicing some customers using technology introduces a two-tier system, those customers that are wealthy enough to warrant human service versus those that do not. This can dilute the private bank's brand. Despite these challenges, many private banks have taken this strategic road, by either collaborating with Robo-advisors (e.g., SigFig collaborating with UBS and Wells Fargo, or True-Wealth collaborating with the Basellandschaftliche Kantonalbank) or acquiring a Robo-advisor (e.g., BinchBank acquiring Pritle or BlackRock acquiring Future Advisor).

2. Value Chain Perspective

Rather than view Robo-advise as a stand-alone offering, the value chain perspective focuses on the specific process steps that can be automated. Robo-advise is seen as a tool for automatically implementing strategic and tactical asset allocations, as well as rebalancing portfolio holdings based on risk analyses. Moreover, it is a well, and sometimes not so well, hidden engine of a holistic investment advice offering (e.g., SimCorp or Charles River). Although such process-automation software systems have recently been termed "Robo-advise", they have existed for more than two decades.

The main challenge faced by the value chain perspective is that it does not cover the entire offering, as seen by the customer. As such, it must deal with numerous interfaces, whether they are data related to customer needs, investment strategy, or portfolios.

3. Customer needs perspective

Rather than trying to fit Robo-advise into an existing strategy, the customer needs perspective aims at following a green-field, customer-driven, approach. It starts by identifying customer needs, their jobs to be done, as Christensen et al. (2016) calls them. The key is to identify the role of the human interactions required by the customer to satisfy his/her needs, which has a lot to do with managing trust and reverting to humans only if and where needed. The main advantage of the customer needs approach is that the Robo-advise strategy does not need to fit into an existing foundation, but rather, it can unfold freely. Further, with this also comes its biggest challenge, acquiring customers. In contrast to the other two perspectives, the customer needs perspective begins with no "a priori" customers at hand.

GAINING COMPETITIVE ADVANTAGE THROUGH FOCUSING

Any successful strategy requires focus, and this is no different for Robo-advisors. To illustrate how a Robo-advisor strategy can compete through focusing, consider the customer needs perspective, which is the most common approach implemented by WealthTech start-ups. Diderich (2016) showed that any successful strategy should be based on one of the following four *strategy views*:

1. *Financials*—Competing on implementing a differentiated pricing model, on superior cost management capabilities, or on both.
2. *Customers*—Focusing on customer needs, suffered pains, and sought-after gains, which cannot be serviced profitably in an offline world, or aiming at those customers that prefer interacting with technology to the human experience.
3. *Offerings*—Aiming at producing and/or delivering investment advice and performance in a completely different and novel way, inventing new models and investment approaches.
4. *Capabilities*—Disintegrating the value chain and focusing on those areas where unique technological capabilities can be exploited, and economies of scale leveraged.

Financial Focus

Many of the existing Robo-advisors have built their strategies, explicitly or implicitly, around price. They offer fees between 0% and 0.75%, the top five averaging 0.19%, whereas Swiss private banks still charge between 1.10% and 1.75% for similar investment solutions (Ruttmann & Ye, 2017). Moreover, some Robo-advisors, like Bloom or Financial Guard, have introduced fixed-fee models. Others are even offering their core Robo-advise services for free, such as Schwab's Intelligent Portfolios solution, cross-financed through the related services and/or fees charged for the use of underlying funds.

Financial based strategies are aimed at both the customers that explicitly buy on price and those that implicitly buy on price, based on whether or not they place value in the investment advice. As with any strategy relying on price as the competitive driver, cost management becomes the predominant differentiator. The underlying logic builds on the causality that cost reductions can be achieved through simplicity, automation, standardization, and the resulting economies of scale. Therefore, whether WealthTech start-ups can compete by relying on a financial-based strategy, especially in a world dominated by big wealth managers and the GAFAMs (Google, Amazon, Facebook, Apple, and Microsoft), with large capital and potential customer bases, remains an open question.

Customer Focus

Wealth managers in the offline world tend to implement customer-focused strategies. For Robo-advisors to compete based on a customer-focused strategy, they need to understand the specifics of the customer needs. Consider a generic value chain underlying an investment advice offering. Figure 24.1 shows the sensitivity of a typical and a millennial customer toward human interaction, allowing

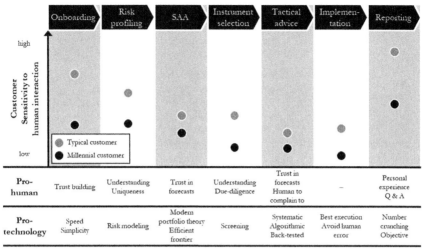

FIGURE 24.1. Typical investment advice value chain identifying the sensitivity of customers to human interaction at each stage

for the understanding of where and why it would make sense to compete with technology rather than human interaction.

Successfully exploiting these insights allows for the designing of a Robo-advise strategy exhibiting a distinct competitive advantage. The strategy should focus on the customer experience along the entire value chain, delivering value for money, providing transparency, and avoiding potential human errors.

Offering Focus

Focusing on offerings is where true innovation comes from. Successful offering-based strategies provide new-to-the-market products and services, satisfying existing and, in some cases, not yet existing customer needs. The challenges with this focus are the highest, but so are the potential rewards. Three key dimensions along which innovation can take place (Ye & McWaters, 2017) are described below:

- *Investment strategy*—Considering new asset classes, segmenting the investment universe in a novel way, and using innovative machine-learning-based forecasting algorithms, are a few examples. Some firms offering innovative solutions focused on investment strategy are Ayasdi (topological data analysis), Kensho (automated investment scenario modeling), Centrifuge Systems (pattern-based business intelligence), and Predixion Software (cloud-based analytics).

- *Risk management*—Introducing new risk measures that better relate to the customer's perception of loss, allocating asset exposures based on risk factors, and adjusting portfolio holdings based on a dynamic definition of risk, are examples in this category. Typical innovative firms competing in the area of risk management are OpenGamma (open-source, real-time risk management), UnRiskOmega (risk visualization), Riskdata (buy-side-driven risk management), and Calypso (integrating risk management and trading).
- *Regulatory requirements*—Transforming regulatory requirements, like MiFID II or PRIPS, into competitive advantage by going the extra mile, using regulations to improve trust with customers, or using transparency to focus on value rather than efforts are some ideas worth pursuing. Firms like Fundapp (cloud-based automated shareholder disclosure), Redkite (real-time fraud, abuse, and manipulation surveillance), Trustev (fraud prevention through real-time transaction scanning), and AQMEtrics (regulatory risk and compliance management) provide innovative solutions that specifically focus on regulations and compliance.

To date, there is no known Robo-advisor in the market that focuses its strategy on offerings. This provides significant opportunities for companies that want to move into this area.

Capabilities Focus

The majority of the existing Robo-advisors, especially those having a relationship with a traditional wealth manager, prefer relying on a capabilities-based strategy, in which existing capabilities are applied to automate some or all of the value chain. In contrast with a customer-based strategy, the focus is on saving time and effort through automation, rather than on offering an optimal customer experience. Existing investment knowledge is combined with technology capabilities to realize both economies of scale and scope. This could, for example, mean replacing one-on-one relationships with one-on-many relationships. Investment strategists can formulate a single investment strategy, which would then, using algorithms, be automatically customized and applied to all customer portfolios, based on their differentiated needs and risk profiles. Alternatively, in-house indexing capabilities could be made available directly to the end customer at a lower cost, making index funds obsolete.

KEY CHALLENGES THAT DETERMINE SUCCESS

A single best strategy for successful Robo-advisors does not exist. But there does exist three key challenges that can make any strategy fail, however innovative it may appear at first sight.

Underestimating Customer Acquisition Costs

Every Robo-advisor, as does any business, needs customers. Customers do not appear just because one is in business, at least most of the time. In fact, acquiring customers has a price. For Robo-advisors of the current generation, analysts estimate average acquisition costs are between USD 300 and USD 1,000 per customer for WealthTech start-ups (Wadhwa, 2016). This is especially relevant to consider if the Robo-advise firm wants to compete on price.

Failing to Show Value to Customers

Customers will choose a Robo-advise offering if the offering can demonstrate that it satisfies their investment needs at a price lower than the value provided. This means that the return after fees must compare favorably to those of competitors, both the traditional wealth managers and other Robo-advisors. As Robo-advisors make predictions about the future, it is important to focus on both the rational and emotional aspects of messaging, trying to build trust in the value-generating capabilities.

Focusing on Automation Over Problem-Solving

No technology, however genius it may be, will make a Robo-advisor successful if it cannot generate value for customers. In other words, technology is usually the easiest challenge to address when launching a Robo-advisor. It is critical to focus on addressing the customer's needs and solving his/her problems before thinking about technology and automation.

CONCLUSION

Many Robo-advisors have failed because they are unable to differentiate themselves from competitors and more traditional offerings in a meaningful way. To be successful, it is critical to understand what makes a Robo-advisor unique and valuable from the customer perspective.

REFERENCES

Brown, T. (2009). *Change by design.* New York, NY: HarperCollins.

CB Insights. (2017). *The global FinTech report Q2 2017.* New York, NY: CB Insights. Retrieved from https://www.cbinsights.com/research/report/fintech-trends-q2-2017/

Christensen, C. M., Hall, T., Dillon, K., & Duncan, D. S. (2016). *Competing against luck.* New York, NY: HarperCollins Publishers.

Diderich, C. (2016). *Initiating the strategy process using design thinking.* 36th Strategic Management Society (SMS) Annual International Conference. Berlin, Germany. Retrieved from https://ssrn.com/abstract=2927941

Ruttmann, R., & Ye, L. (2017). Why Robo-Advisory is the way forward for wealth management. *Wealth Advice*. Retrieved from Redesigning Financial Services: https://redesigning-fs.com/assets/img/pdf/publication-wealth-advice-2017-01.pdf

Wadhwa, T. (2016). One of the hottest investment styles might be 'financially unviable.' *Business Insider UK*. Retrieved from http://uk.businessinsider.com/robo-advisors-may-be-financially-unviable-2016-7?r=US&IR=T

Ye, L., & McWaters, R. J. (2017). Taxonomy of new business models in wealth managment. *Wealth Advice*. Retrieved from https://redesigning-fs.com/assets/img/pdf/publication-wealth-advice-2017-01.pdf

PART 10

THE HUMAN SIDE OF WEALTHTECH

CHAPTER 25

AGE OF DISCOVERY

Navigating the Balance
Between Human and Machine

Dimitrios Salampasis, Anne-Laure Mention, and Alexander Kaiser

Wealth management is experiencing transformational changes. Advisory services are embedded within a human to human interaction and robo-advising is going to augment the existing value chain leading to the creation of a hybrid advisory model for complex investment portfolios. Therefore, the fundamental question is not about either or but together for ...

INTRODUCTION

With the pace of change accelerating in the world around us, technology has ramped up competition. The emergence of innovative technology-enabled business models constantly forces incumbent financial institutions to clarify their strategies, to develop new capabilities and to transform their cultures. The asset and wealth management industry is thus being pushed towards a 'disruptive' advancement.

New tools such as screeners, tech chart analysis, opportunities for high frequency trading and research-based advice support active trading. If the client is

WealthTech: Wealth and Asset Management in the FinTech Age, pages 167–174.

correctly positioned in a risk suitability model, automated advice can be generated.

FinTech as "a new financial industry that applies technology to improve financial activities" (Schueffel, 2016, p. 45) is built upon distributed models in terms of bringing technology closer and allowing the development of new services, encouraging customer value and centricity. FinTech brings along an entirely different logic that is causing fundamental changes in the structure and purpose of business. It introduces changes that the majority of incumbents are still not ready to face. In this frame of reference, the impact of WealthTech as a subset of FinTech is primarily seen in finding new ways of meeting changing customer needs with new offerings by better understanding customers' behavior and expectations, and therefore incumbents are looking for new ways to partner for innovation.

This article aims at shedding light on the role of Robo-advisors (being one aspect of WealthTech) as an emerging service innovation element within the wealth management industry. The authors argue that the industry is currently experiencing transformational changes with regards to client interaction and customer onboarding, along with a cultural shift in customer relationship practices. Advisory services are embedded within a human to human interaction and robo-advising will augment the existing value chain but not replace the human component. Therefore, the fundamental question is not about either or but together for ...

WEALTH MANAGEMENT AND TECHNOLOGY

Revolutionary developments in technology are creating a transformational shift in the way the marketplace for investment products and services is currently functioning, incrementally changing the business of investing and managing of wealth, generating a 'purely' technological investing experience. The primary innovation lies within the introduction of a 'disintermediation' scenario that aims at developing an alternative wealth management business model characterized by automation. Individual investors have the ability to proceed with 'do-it-by-yourself' investing actions directly without the advice/presence of an investment advisor, broker or other intermediary financial services institution. They do so by the means of pre-programmed models and parameters used as the basis for digital service or automated wealth management service models, i.e. Robo-advisors (Crager & Hummel, 2016). Moreover, this emerging advisory marketplace, which is heavily capitalizing on the numerous opportunities that technological growth provides, aims at offering 'personal financial management to the vast majority of the population. It thus also targets a segment that otherwise falls below the net worth threshold required by many banking and brokerage institutions which provide human-driven wealth management services' (Gold & Kursh, 2017, p. 140).

THE EMERGENCE OF ROBO-ADVISORS

Technology is positioned in the heart of these cataclysmic changes leading to the emergence of new propositions and innovative streams of offerings that the wealth management industry cannot ignore anymore. One of these fundamental changes is related to the looming form of algorithmic advisors, respectively Robo-advisors. In an innovative fashion Robo-advisors combine discretionary decision-making and artificial intelligence. Nested within these technological breakthroughs, yet behind and even beyond human intelligence, Robo-advisors aim at generating alpha by eliminating irrational decisions via automated index-investing strategies which exclude human psychology and emotional vulnerability (Tertilt & Scholz, 2017). Baker and Dellaert (2017, p. 1) suggest that a Robo-advisor refers to 'any automated service that ranks, or matches consumers, to financial products on a personalized basis, sometimes in addition to providing related services, such as educating consumers and selling products to them'. Robo-advisors usually display the following key elements: a) provision of full digital access, b) performance of automated portfolio rebalancing, c) adoption of indexation or passive management and d) personalization aligned to customers' goals and behavior (Sironi, 2016). The pendulum of transformation of service delivery within the wealth management industry is ticking under an unprecedented pace and the rising powers of non-human decision-making 'anatomies' are not considered as a science fiction any longer.[1]

Human advisors are required to consider a person's investment objectives, financial situation, and particular needs in the process of providing recommendations for investment products. Robo-advisory mechanisms are based on a 'controlled rationality' investment logic that allows the performance of a finite number of algorithmic calculations and asset allocation models based on proprietary historical data (vast quantities of big data). In addition, typically means-variance optimization is applied in order to define the optimal solution tailored to each individual investor's needs under certain conditions, specific circumstances and within a definite point in time.[2] In simple terms, Robo-advisors function within a 'limitations-of-algorithm' framework that is based on the information the individual investor provides. The determination of what is best, flawless or 'gilt-edge' is determined by the execution of automated rationalized and analytical processes towards impartial and 'logical' outcomes. However, this raises a number of questions particularly around assumptions that can be deemed as incorrect or inapplicable to the financial situation of an individual investor based on superficial information or lack of psychometrics (Tertilt & Scholz, 2017). Furthermore, erroneous assumptions could potentially lead to a 'mismatch between a Robo-advisor's recommendations and the clients' actual financial planning horizon' (Huxley & Kim,

---

[1] Tammas-Hastings (2017) believes that the term 'semi-automated digital guiders' is more accurate.

[2] Huxley and Kim (2016, p.10) argue that 'the mapping of client's responses to robo-advisor portfolios appears to be very shortsighted with respect to the timing of when clients plan to spend their money'.

2016, p. 2) It even cannot be ruled out that the client is provided 'canned' asset allocation offerings and investment recommendations (Fein, 2015).

Trust, long-term and predictive analytics are the key inherent elements of advisory services in managing wealth. An advisor aims at building a long-lasting, continuous, and trustworthy relationships. He or she does so with existing but also new customers by anticipating and envisioning change in a pro-active rather than a reactive manner, especially in times of volatility. Robo-advisors are able to monitor personal needs and market conditions, while providing automated advice for portfolio rebalancing. Human advisory is based on emotional intelligence fostering rigorous decision-making with impact.

The human advisor synthesizes controlled and uncontrolled rationality, along with controlled and uncontrolled irrationality principles, also known as 'gut feeling'. The human nature is a complex collage of behavioral norms, individual peculiarities and capabilities that simultaneously interact with the internal and the external environment. The human principles within the advisory process depend on the various psychological and socio-cultural contexts, therefore, impartiality is not always guaranteed. On the other hand, impartiality is one of the most fundamental elements within the 'machinized' advisory paradigm, where datasets and historical testimonies aim at creating new ways of advisory delivery for solid and unprejudiced decision-making.

Robo-advisory is bringing new elements of innovation within the wealth management value chain by providing augmented offerings. These offerings may either collaborate with the existing business functions or may even eliminate the human component entirely by using automated and artificial processes. Ultimately, they are likely to incorporate patterns for generating 'dehumanized' content or even non-human decision-making standards. This model is constantly exploring direct causal and relational archetypes for neutral, unbiased and objective predictabilities beyond human irrationality.

One fundamental element behind the emergence of Robo-advisors is the 'technological neutrality' principle. This level refers to the following questions: 'who is responsible for what'? and 'who has reputational incentives for what?'. This element has created numerous discussions around the need for revisiting and revising investment advice regulations. Singapore,[3] Hong Kong,[4] United States,[5] and United Kingdom[6] have recently issued a number of consultation papers touching upon that topic.

---

[3] Monetary of Authority, Provision of Digital Advisory Services Consultation Paper (June, 2017).

[4] Securities and Futures Commission, Consultation Paper on the Proposed Guidelines on Online Distribution and Advisory Platforms (May 2017).

[5] SEC, Division of Investment Management, Guidance Update on Robo-advisers (February, 2017).

[6] Financial Conduct Authority, Financial Advice Market Review (FAMR) Guidance Consultation (April, 2017).

BALANCING HUMAN AND MACHINE

The emergence of Robo-advisors leads to a crucial question revolving around the balance between the human and the machine components in the advisory and the decision-making process in wealth management. The authors believe that there is a need for wealth managers to choose the right mix of automated analysis and human intervention in order to make better decisions within the investment decision-making realm. Moreover, the authors argue that despite the fact that it is growing[7] the computer-led investment advisory model will always embed the human component.

The evolution of this model will be a hybrid co-existence between the human and the machine spheres (Figure 25.1). The 'Robo' element will help augmenting the existing wealth management value chain by complementing rather than displacing the human advisory function. Wealth management is all about building a personal advisory relationship providing personalized investment guidance to individual investors. Artificial intelligence is not able to provide 'advisory' services because advisory means ability to connect, ability to interpret data and ability to adopt abductive reasoning to help the investor reach out to a decision. The semi-automated digital guiders can bring innovation to the service provision but are not able to advise and connect to the investor in an emotional intelligence manner, taking also into account the social, cultural, and psychological and political contexts.

The authors do not fully agree with Bussmann (2017) who believes that the emphasis is shifting towards relationship management while leaving the machine to provide the advice by implementing sophisticated investment strategies. Machines will be able to execute numerous sophisticated calculations by synthesiz-

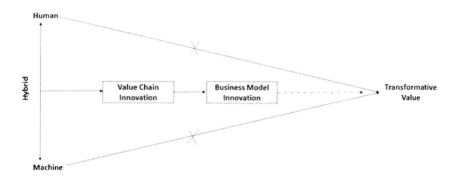

FIGURE 25.1.   Hybrid Co-Existence (developed by the authors)

---

[7] There are many reasons behind this growth including social and political factors, along with, an increased regulatory focus on incumbent wealth management institutions, however, the exploration of these reasons go beyond the scope of this book chapter.

ing enormous amount of data and parameters, but the human advisor will still be
holding the key to unlocking the decision-making process by helping the investor
reach the final decision. Therefore, Robo-advisors cannot generate decisions for
the investor. Rather than that the Robo-advisor will assist the human financial
advisor in guiding the investor towards the optimal decision.

WHAT IS NEXT FOR THIS HYBRID CO-EXISTENCE?

The technological developments within the wealth management industry are undoubtedly bringing anticipated changes in investing behavior. Moreover, an immense boost of productivity of the wealth management sector is expected by the
introduction of Robo-advisors.

The traditional discretionary mandate is based on an individual profile and
implements the chosen asset allocation with a constructed portfolio. Changes
in markets lead to re-assessment and re-balancing. This process is already automated to a large degree in today's banking world. Nonetheless, better tools in
the Robo-advise space will support better and swifter implementation of a better
customized investment profile. These mandates are traditionally for clients with
bankable assets greater that USD 1m. Robo-advise is expected to significantly
lower this threshold. Robo-advisors will help to significantly push these limits
down towards smaller customers' accounts. Hence, the affluent segment holding approximately USD 500k per client will benefit greatly from the increased
productivity. Theoretically, if fully equipped with the right Robo-advisory tools,
relationship managers are furnished with the technology of a small bank. In this
scenario, semi-actively managed asset pools of USD 2bn per relationship manager could become realistic. The combination of collaborative approaches, where
the financial intermediary has access to customer driven inputs (from Robo-advise usage) and behavioural data could help to further increase the quality of an
existing investment as well as future ones. It could help to adjust more precise to
the risk profile of the client.

The combinative forces of human and machine principles create numerous opportunities, while at the same time pose many challenges. The hybrid model of
advisory in managing wealth will lead towards a redefinition of what true value
means both for the advisor and the investor yet it will enhance and extend human
performance. In particular, the authors see two major changes in this emerging
landscape:

1. Redefinition of Wealth Management

The authors believe that the traditional 'business as usual' practices in wealth
management will experience a transformational shift as wealth management will
be presented a range of new investment opportunities. The principles of desirability, feasibility, and viability of the provided advisory services are crafted
within the sphere of 'acceptance'. The investment decision-making process will

now be reflected within a spectrum of algorithms, rationality, irrationality, ethical decision-making, and behavioral management elements. In principle, the wealth management culture is bound to become more inclusive and more democratized providing a wider range of different advises to a larger group of customers at varying fees levels. The main challenge hereby is the quality of the advice provided, the trustworthiness of the institution, and how the generated advice captures all the necessary elements of human and machine intelligence in order to foster approval, popularity and status. The introduction of 'robo' in the advisory process creates different levels of human and computational capabilities that need to be properly orchestrated. Only then the advisory process can efficiently support and influence the decision of the investor based on the individual distinctive peculiarities, characteristics and circumstances of the individual.

2. Changes in the Profile of the Advisor and Investor

This transformational shift will be creating a new cohort of advisors and investors. There is a need for focusing on cultivating soft skills in order to facilitate client relationships and communications. This re-focus of attention must be complemented with assembling the right training and talent acquisition and retention mechanisms to support human advisors in the integration process with the artificial intelligence elements. Moreover, we expect the investors to become more educated by demonstrating increased skills, expertise, and ethical focus in their investment process. This is necessary to build a sustainable investing ecosystem supported by the combinative co-existence of human and artificial intelligence principles that will have a dynamic effect on the investor's decision-making process.

CONCLUDING REMARKS

The complexity in financial advice is becoming more and more sophisticated, leading to groundbreaking changes in traditional finance. Investors' decision-making processes can be affected by human emotions, cognitive or idiosyncratic biases—elements that are going to be reduced by the use of Robo-advisors. However, complexity can be both intensive and extensive, therefore the combinative forces of robo and human advisory need to be mobilized in order to provide desirable, feasible, and viable advice on these complex investment portfolios. Many questions still remain unanswered, however the age of discovery within the hybrid wealth management advisory has already begun.

REFERENCES

Baker, T., & Dellaert, B. (2017). *Regulating robo advisors: Old policy goals, new challenges* (p. 47). Penn Wharton Public Policy Initiative. Retrieved from: http://repository.upenn.edu/pennwhartonppi/47

Brown, N. P. (2016). *Culture, communication, and the next generation of investors, Advisor Perspectives*, November, Greenwood Village, CO: Investment Management Consultant Association. Retrieved from: https://www.advisorperspectives.com/commentaries/2016/11/28/culture-communication-and-the-next-generation-of-investors.pdf

Bussmann O. (2017) The future of finance: FinTech, tech disruption, and orchestrating innovation. In Francioni R., & Schwartz R. (Eds.), *Equity markets in transition*. Cham: Springer.

Crager, B., & Hummel, J. (2016). The essential advisor: *Building value in the investor-advisor relationship*. Hoboken, NJ: John Wiley & Sons.

Fein, M. L. (June 30, 2015). *Robo-advisors: A closer look*. Available at SSRN: https://ssrn.com/abstract=2658701 or http://dx.doi.org/10.2139/ssrn.2658701

Financial Conduct Authority. (2017). *Guidance consultation: GC17/4—Financial Advice Market Review (FAMR): Implementation part 1*. Retrieved from: https://www.fca.org.uk/publication/guidance-consultation/gc17-04.pdf

Gold, N. A., & Kursh, S. R. (2017). Counterrevolutionaries in the financial services industry: Teaching disruption–A case study of roboadvisors and incumbent responses. *Business Education Innovation Journal, 9*(1), 139–146.

Huxley, S. J., & Kim, J. Y. (2016). *The short-term nature of robo portfolios. Advisor perspectives*. September, Greenwood Village, CO: Investment Management Consultant Association. Retrieved from: https://www.advisorperspectives.com/articles/2016/09/12/the-short-term-nature-of-robo-portfolios.pdf

Schueffel, P. (2016). Taming the beast: A scientific definition of FinTech. *Journal of Innovation Management, 4*(4), 32–54.

SEC. (2016). *Update guidance on robo-advisers*. Retrieved from: https://www.sec.gov/investment/im-guidance-2017-02.pdf

Securities and Futures Commission. (2017). *Consultation paper on the proposed guidelines on online distribution and advisory platforms*. Retrieved from: https://www.sfc.hk/edistributionWeb/gateway/EN/consultation/openFile?refNo=17CP3

Sironi, P. (2016). My robo advisor was an iPod—Applying the lessons from other sectors to fintech disruption. In S. Chishti & J. Barberis (Eds.), *The FinTech book: The financial technology handbook for investors, entrepreneurs and visionaries* (pp. 152–154). Hoboken, NJ: Wiley.

Tammas-Hastings, D. (2017). 'WealthTech': The challenges facing the wealth management industry. *LSE Business Review*. Retrieved from: http://eprints.lse.ac.uk/83218/1/LSE%20Business%20Review%20%E2%80%93%20%E2%80%98WealthTech%E2%80%99_%20The%20challenges%20facing%20the%20wealth%20management%20industry.pdf

Tertilt, M., & Scholz, P. (June 12, 2017). *To advise, or not to advise—How robo-advisors evaluate the risk preferences of private investors*. Retrieved from SSRN: https://ssrn.com/abstract=2913178

CHAPTER 26

A CALL FOR MORE CASE STUDIES ON FINTECH INNOVATION

Wolfgang Amann

Business schools and the executive learning community rely on case studies to keep track of changes and update 'mental software,'. These unique learning tools are especially important for business environments that are in flux. This paper highlights the need for case studies in the areas of FinTech and WealthTech. It points which findings from case development should be applied to these areas and issues a call to develop more cases.

LIVING IN THE AGE OF THE END OF MANAGEMENT MODELS

Across industries, and especially in the financial services sector, CEOs of established companies need to cope with disruption. In the financial services sector, non-traditional players will easily generate up to 40% of revenues within the next 10 years. The fundamental sources of value creation and competitive advantage are shifting. This disruption categorizes companies into three groups: Those that make things happen, those that watch things happen, and those that wondered what happened!

WealthTech: Wealth and Asset Management in the FinTech Age, pages 175–182.

In order to keep track of changes and update 'mental software,' business schools and the executive learning community need to rely on the latest case studies. They are a unique tools for our business environments in flux. A case might well be made against the normal long time that it takes to develop new management models for the fast-paced FinTech world. If we were still living in simple times, the role of guidelines and checklists to ensure success in the financial services sector would still be essential. This would be like having a successful recipe for simple tasks, such as baking a cake. No real experts or expertise would be required. Even more, the repeatability of success would be ensured. Alas, we no longer live in simple times! Our approaches to sustainable success need to be different in a complicated world. Missions, such as putting a man on the moon, require detailed checklists and a disciplined organizational culture. Experts are needed to effectively execute plans and to monitor then closely. But even then, success is not always guaranteed.

We do live in complicated times. The high rate of fundamental disruption is indicative of complex times and business environments. Simplistic checklists are as counterproductive as they would be for raising a child. Experts and their expertise would only be beneficial if they could also learn fast what will be happening next. Yet, the repeatability of success is very low. What works with child number one may not necessarily and automatically be right for child number two. In the corporate world and financial services sector, Deutsche Bank's former CEO Josef Ackermann is a case in point. Despite his, at times, extreme investment and leadership approaches, including investment models in slum real estates, money laundering, gold price fixing, laying off 18% of the staff, selling EUR 11bn. in assets,[1] he did not reach the set and agreed upon strategic objectives. Whatever efficiency gains he implemented, competition and turbulent economic conditions caught up with him. While the aftermath of the 2008 global financial crisis can still be felt, the next drivers of flux, namely technological changes, challenge established solutions. In light of this business context, simplistic management models—a two-by-two matrix à la BCG, or three-by-three matrix à la McKinsey—simply no longer apply. The world and its trends have become too ambiguous to extract general models from them.

This is not a fatalistic situation: Case studies are a tool with which we can capture, study, and thus practice our mental problem-solving muscles. Learning does not address general, universal, cross-cultural, cross-industry, cross-ownership types of organizations, but situational, temporary patterns. Case studies address a variety of problems more adequately than management models can. There are at least three types of problems: First, puzzle problems—although they might be rather challenging—have a fundamental and stable structure. Regardless of how many pieces there are and their colors, there is one way of solving them. There are either-or decisions to be taken—to allocate a piece here or there, but clearly not

---

[1] Cf. http://www.referenceforbusiness.com/biography/A-E/Ackermann-Josef-1948.html

both. More importantly, we can be certain that there is indeed a solution; we simply have to make an effort to find it. Experts, experienced individuals, and teams can help with more complicated puzzles. We have a variety of solutions in place to address puzzle problems effectively. We could use trial and error, structuring, chunking, framing, clustering, etc. Based on experience, we can also predict the time required to solve it.

Wicked problems, in turn, need time to simply be understood properly. And by the time the analysis has been done, the nature of the issue and the organizational internal and external environments might well have evolved to a critical degree. Similar to dilemmas and trilemmas, proactively finding and perfectly implementing a truly satisfactory, considerate solution becomes virtually impossible. When urgent solutions are needed, case studies can help train executives to feel more comfortable with this new reality, to embrace complexity, and overcome the risk of paralysis through analysis. Case studies can reflect the messiness, the relevant players' perceptions, the rich details of a situational dilemma in a specific context, and the sense of urgency needed in the real world. The next section outlines how truly good executive education providers integrate case studies into their unique learning journeys.

CASE STUDIES AS THE CENTERPIECE FOR HIGH IMPACT EXECUTIVE EDUCATION

Some business schools, especially Anglo-Saxon ones, grant a too dominant position to case studies in executive education seminars and do not embed them in a more conducive learning environment. Great executive education providers do critically reflect upon the use of case studies. They view case studies as a means to an end, not as an end in themselves. They understand that four key learning styles must be respected and served,[2] as shown in the following figure. They even create transparency on how executives can learn, which is an additional benefit of attending such seminars. The four emerging learning styles and learner types can be structured along two dimensions: the perception dimension, as well as the information processing perception:

- In the perception dimension, learners grow through either concrete experiences, or more abstract input.
- Regarding the information processing dimension, learners may prefer to actively experiment with a subject matter or rely on reflective observation.

If we want to use case studies in executive education seminars, it helps to understand whom we are teaching. If a large number of reflectors are present, much time and energy should be allocated to reflection. Most case study and executive

---

[2] Cf.   https://www2.le.ac.uk/departments/gradschool/training/eresources/teaching/theories/honey-mumford

education seminar models suggest that all four learning styles have benefits their benefits:

- Activists should receive the opportunity to work on a solution, experiment with tools, and defend their answers in front of a reasonably critical, yet constructive, audience.
- Reflectors should obtain crystal clear messages from the case. Reflectors should therefore not be faced with many, often very lengthy Harvard style cases, where the problem is hidden. The case writing philosophy at IMD, where cases are better tailored to the busy executives would be better. If the course participants read the first page and the last, they will understand most of the issues. The problems are clear, which means the emphasis can be on finding solutions, resulting in clear messages.
- Theorists are also found among practicing leaders and managers. This label refers to the interest of this type of learner, who can understand concepts cognitively.
- Finally, pragmatists would ideally want to skip lengthy debates and focus on the three things they need to do after reading the case and returning to their workplace. This again favors shorter case studies, not the typical 25-page Harvard case with numerous appendices and exhibits.

By the means of this paper, a call is issued to develop more cases on the Fin-Tech industry in general and on WealthTech in particular. If published as stand-

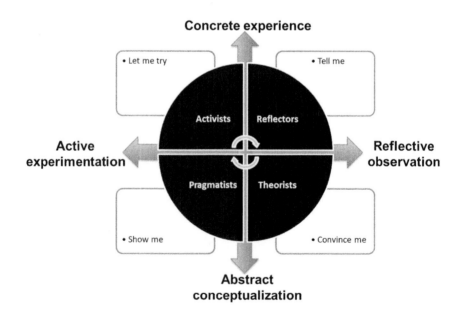

FIGURE 26.1.   Key Learning Styles in the Honey-Mumford Typology

alone pieces, they need to be embedded in further explanations on why the topic is important. Because no course faculty members are present when the readers work their way through the cases, reflections have to be made explicit, as well as the key conceptual considerations and major lessons to be learned. These allow all four learning types to be satisfied. The next section of this paper sheds more light on what actually makes a good case. I consequently draw on my experiences with writing more than a hundred case studies for executive education, with my case writing workshops held around the world, with serving in juries of key case writing competitions, and with previously publishing case writing guides.[3]

CORNERSTONES OF EFFECTIVE CASE STUDIES

The quality of a case determines the degree to which a reader is hooked and actually finishes it. Interestingly enough, in ancient Greece, storytelling was already a perfect art. The Greek Golden Rules of Storytelling are still the backbone of key fiction novels, Hollywood/Bollywood/Nollywood movies, and executive education case studies. The major elements of Greek storytelling are summarized in the following and illustrated in the figure below. Case studies come in all forms, lengths, and for a variety of purposes. They usually share these key elements.

1. The protagonist: Each case must adopt a clear perspective. Does an individual decide, or a group, or multiple stakeholders? Especially when it comes to FinTech and WealthTech case studies, it might be tempting to fall in love with technology, its amazing innovative power, as well as its bells and whistles. However, we continue to live in socio-technical systems and, therefore, must understand how these technologies can add value, find acceptance, or shift the deliverables of the involved humans, such as the analysts, enablers, and clients.

2. The goal: A case must be straightforward concerning the goals relating to the protagonist, the company, the board, or society. This is why cases often end with key questions, for instance, should person X decide in favor or against a certain plan or not?

3. The obstacles: Every case must be clear on at least some of the obstacles deterring the protagonist and allies from achieving a goal.

4. The struggle: Good cases elaborate on the flow of events between different episodes, including the origin of a dilemma as the steps unfold, potentially leading to a crisis. Cases describing wrongdoings should be reasonably clear on the damage that is either caused, or expected, due to decisions that need to be taken.

---

[3] Cf., for example, Adler, G. and W. Amann (2001). Case writing for executive education: a survival guide. IAP.

5. The context: The reader must have sufficient details of the context in which court decisions need be taken, or in which a dilemma unfolded, for instance, the relevant regulations, or the costs of wrongdoings.

6. The delivery style: Cases must be well written, in the active voice, and they should only be long enough to ensure that the reader does not lose interest, or develop paralysis through analysis, i.e. when too much information needs to be processed.

7. The lessons: The faculty aiming to use the case must be clear on the lessons it should bring to the classroom. The case author with practitioners in mind as the target group must also converge on key insights. Additional ideas might emerge at any point during the case discussion, but the top three lessons that a case study must convey should be known ex ante.

The last point in the timeline is a case study's natural cutoff point. Beyond positioning a case in terms of the target audience and the complexity level, case authors must decide where to position their cases in a typical decision-making process. When using cases to combat wrongdoings and especially corruption, these points should be addressed carefully.

Complying with the Greek Golden Rules of Storytelling is not enough to write efficient and effective case studies. As an additional checklist, we should look for the four learning outcomes discussed next. They kick-off with essential insights to be gained on the 'knowing' level. What is it about company X, innovation Y,

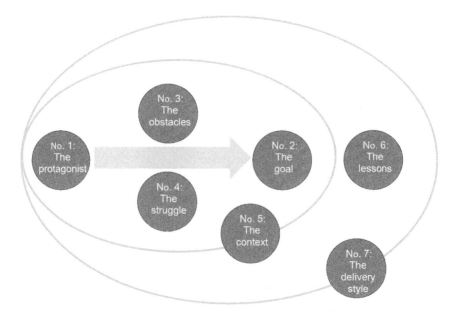

FIGURE 26.2.   Elements of the Greek Golden Rules of Storytelling

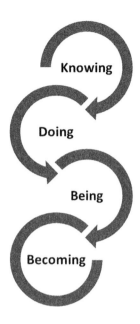

FIGURE 26.3.   Key Learning Outcomes

or customer segment Z that the reader should understand? A good case enables progress on this level.

Learning should not be limited to 'knowing' but comprise progress on the 'doing' level. How can project managers or executives implement such solutions? If we adopt an investor's perspective, what are the special factors to consider for the idea in a case to work in the future, or if it has been successfully implemented? What actionable knowledge can be gained for implementing solutions effectively?

As illustrated in the following figure, the learning does not stop here. A good case study integrates lessons to be learnt on the 'being' level. What kind of Fin-Tech executive, or project manager, do we aspire to be? What kind of ethical questions emerge and what is our stance on them? The United Nations Principles of Responsible Management Education (PRME), as well as the Global Compact for the corporate world, aim at fully integrating ethical and sustainability considerations into educational debates and material. Without the 'being' level, great cases would simply be incomplete.

The same is true of the fourth level—the 'becoming'. Case studies should not be limited to short-term, quick-wins. They should enable holistic, longer-term, or at least multi-stage development. Rome was not built in a day. It is unlikely that an established player in the financial services sector will get rid of all existing resources and undertake a system shift in the blink of an eye. This is even less likely to be the case in the WealthTech area where firms oftentimes rely on long-term client relationships. FinTech and especially WealthTech companies should also not be portrayed as a one-trick dog. Evidence of further ideas and the potential for further trajectories over time can help readers more fully understand what an organization can do. Great cases are not limited to one-time solutions. Shedding light on multiple trajectories over time should not be limited to technology alone, but comprise aspects related to key stakeholders.

CONCLUSIONS

In the Fall of 2019, when this chapter was written, TheCaseCentre.org, one of the most prominent online case clearing houses for case studies, only offered 42 fresh case studies written during the past three years. They clearly do not sufficiently depict the highly diverse, fast-moving universe of newly established FinTech and WealthTech players and responses from 'the establishment'. More effort and more diverse case writing efforts are needed to share emerging, situational patterns and solutions through case studies. These case studies should also shed more light on the local and cultural backgrounds in which they are placed. FinTech and Wealth-Tech, like many other innovations, needs to more pervasively enter executive education, and we need fresh material to help executives cope with the adversity and opportunities ahead. This chapter outlined the importance of case studies in such educational efforts, how cases can help satisfy different learner types, and what constitutes a good case (while explicitly requesting an integration of ethical, societal considerations and the 'being' level). In the ideal case scenario, we will see a diverse set of new cases being produced in the months and years to come— very much along the lines outlined in this chapter.

ABOUT THE AUTHORS

ABOUT THE EDITOR

Patrick Schueffel is adjunct professor at the Institute of Finance at Fribourg's School of Management. His research interests focus on the areas of Entrepreneurship in Banking & Finance, Innovation, and International Business. He has published widely in academic as well as practitioner journals in Switzerland and internationally. Prior to his academic career Professor Schueffel held various senior positions at banks in Switzerland. Among others he served as the Chief Operating Officer of Saxo Bank Switzerland and as a director at Credit Suisse's Private Banking Division. He holds a doctorate degree from Henley Business School at the University of Reading/UK, a master's degree from the Norwegian School of Economics and Diploma from Mannheim University/Germany.

CONTRIBUTORS AND AFFILIATIONS

Dr. Wolfgang Amann: Professor and Academic Director HEC Paris, Qatar

Maurizio Ballesteros>Director Strategic Planning and New Business Development at Banregio, Adj. Professor ITESM, Monterrey/Mexcio

WealthTech: Wealth and Asset Management in the FinTech Age, pages 183–185.

Steffen Bassler: Managing Director Switzerland Capstan Capital Partners LLP, Zurich/Switzerland and Business Development Executive SwissOne Capital AG, Zug/Switzerland

Marc P. Bernegger: Co-founder Finance 2.0, Board Member at Crypto Finance AG, Greater Zurich Area and Falcon Private Bank, Zurich/Switzerland

Jean Bonnefoy: Partner Périclès Group, Paris/France

Nicolas Buerkler: Lecturer Lucerne University of Applied Sciences and Arts, member of the advisory board of Bros Partners, Zug/Switzerland

J. P. Caldeira: Executive at Noosa Technology & Finance, Evooqee and Edge Laboratories, Lausanne/Switzerland

Dr. Felix Cardenas: Board Member EFM Capital, President and Managing Partner BlueBox Ventures, Director Center for Innovation and Corporate Entrepreneurship EGADE Business School, Monterrey/Mexico

Raphael Cretinon: Partner Périclès Group, Paris/France

Claude Diderich: Founder and Managing Director, innovate.d llc, Richterswil/Switzerland

Hendrik Emrich: CEO and Founder Portal 72, Hamburg/Germany

Floyd DCosta: Co-Founder and Managing Director, Blockchain Worx, Singapore

Daniel Fasnacht: CEO at Ecosystem Partners AG, Zollikon/Switzerland Head Wealth & Asset Management at Business Engineering Institute St. Gallen AG, St.Gallen/Switzerland

David Gyori: CEO Banking Reports, London/UK

Nicholas Hochstadter: Founder & CEO of Performance Watcher by IBO, Morges/Switzerland

Dr. Claus Huber: Project Manager and Portfolio Manager at Deka Investment GmbH, Frankfurt/Germany and Managing Director Rodex Risk Advisers, Altendorf/Switzerland

Alexander Kaiser: Director of the Australian Graduate School of Entrepreneurship at the Swinburne University of Technology, Melbourne/Australia

Dr. Ulf Klebeck: General Counsel at Montana Capital Partners AG, Zurich/Switzerland

Dr. Richard-Marc Lacasse: Professor at Université du Québec à Rimouski (UQAR), Lévis/Canada

Dr. Berthe Lambert: Professor at Université du Québec à Rimouski (UQAR), Lévis/Canada

Richard B. Levin: Shareholder and Chair of the FinTech and Regulation Practice at Polsinelli PC, Denver/USA

Gregory Mall: Portfolio Manager at SEBA Bank AG, Zurich/Switzerland

Dr. Anne-Laure Mention: Director Global Business Innovation Enabling Capability Platform and Professor at the School of Management at RMIT University, Melbourne/Australia

Dr. Dietmar Peetz: Partner at Systematic Investment Management AG, Zurich/Switzerland

Torsten Ries: Member of the Management Board and Head Private Equity & Real Estate at VP Fund Solutions, Luxembourg

Dr. Dimitrios Salampasis: Lecturer Swinburne Business School, Swinburne University of Technology, Melbourne/Australia

Anna Schmid: Senior Strategist at Institute for Applied Risk Analysis (IFARA), Zurich/Switzerland

Nicolas Steiner: Director Strategy and Innovation - EMEA & APAC at Invesco Ltd., Partner I4E, London/UK

Helena Steiner: Director Business Development TallyFox Social Technologies AG, Zurich/Switzerland⁻

Alexander Tomenendal: Director Financial Services Technology at EXXETA, Frankfurt/Germany

Maryna Tykholoz-Cukov: Client Manager Private Banking at Credit Suisse, Zurich/Switzerland

Peter F. Waltz: Attorney at Polsinelli PC, Denver/USA

Robert W. Wenner: Associate at Polsinelli, Denver, USA

Printed in Great Britain
by Amazon